Finding Jesus in Jeremiah

A Study of the Book of Jeremiah for Small Groups

Cheryl Bongiorno

WESTBOW
PRESS®
A DIVISION OF THOMAS NELSON
& ZONDERVAN

Scripture taken from the Holy Bible, NEW INTERNATIONAL VERSION®. Copyright © 1973, 1978, 1984 by Biblica, Inc. All rights reserved worldwide. Used by permission. NEW INTERNATIONAL VERSION® and NIV® are registered trademarks of Biblica, Inc. Use of either trademark for the offering of goods or services requires the prior written consent of Biblica US, Inc.

WestBow Press books may be ordered through booksellers or by contacting:

WestBow Press
A Division of Thomas Nelson & Zondervan
1663 Liberty Drive
Bloomington, IN 47403
www.westbowpress.com
1 (866) 928-1240

ISBN: 978-1-5127-0145-6 (sc)
ISBN: 978-1-5127-0146-3 (e)

Print information available on the last page.

WestBow Press rev. date: 12/29/2015

CONTENTS

PREFACE

Jeremiah is one of many great prophets in the Bible. Yet, few people know much about him, because it requires some effort to read through the fifty-two chapters of his book. The chapters are not chronological, so it can be confusing, and adding to the confusion are the complicated times Jeremiah lived in. Judah (the only part of Israel that still existed during Jeremiah's lifetime), was ruled by five different kings during Jeremiah's forty years of prophetic ministry.

My purpose in writing this study is to introduce Jeremiah to those who haven't yet read His book. I hope to bring clarity to the prophetic message by reorganizing the chapters into chronological order, and by focusing on one portion of scripture each day. If you have not spent much time reading through the Old Testament history or the prophets, this book will provide a good introductory study of the kings and prophets of Israel. Small groups will enjoy discovering the great truths in the book of Jeremiah together.

"Jeremiah is the quintessential prophet for the postmodern age. He provides us with an extended study of an era like our own, where men have turned away from God and the society has become post-Christian". (Schaeffer: Death of a City, 1969)

Jeremiah's message is relevant to all believers in this 21st century. He lived through the "last days" of Israel before they went into captivity. He watched and observed his people turn their backs on God, and knew that they were heading for disaster. He modeled for us how we are to live in a corrupt world, and yet not be a part of it.

Jeremiah pointed our attention to Jesus Christ, the Messiah. Jesus told His followers that they too should be watching the events around them. He told us to look forward with excitement to His triumphant return. This is our blessed hope.

Jesus said,

> *"And this gospel of the kingdom will be preached in the whole world as a testimony to all nations, and then the end will come." Matthew 24:14*

> *"No one knows about that day or hour...learn a lesson from the fig tree: As soon as its twigs get tender and its leaves come out, you will know that summer is near. Even so, when you see all these things, you know that it is near, right at the door." Matthew 24:32-33, 36*

Jeremiah was alive to witness the fulfillment of many of his own prophecies. He sadly stood and watched as the City of David (Jerusalem) went up in flames. God was faithful to keep His Word to Jeremiah. Knowing that God kept His Word encourages us to believe what Jesus said regarding His future return. I can trust God to keep His promises, because I know He is faithful, and His Word is true. God's faithfulness to keep His Word is a sub-theme throughout this study.

You will find that the order of the chapters in this study and those in your Bible do not line up, which can be confusing if you are attempting to bookmark your Bible pages. We will follow the chapters chronologically according to the historical events and the information taken right from the Scripture itself. We may not know the exact year, but we can identify which king was in power, and we can use the Book of Chronicles and Kings to help us organize the events as they happen. We will be reading from both Old and New Testaments, finding similarities between the teachings of Jesus and Jeremiah. The New International Version was used for all of the questions and answers, including "fill in the blanks", so it would be helpful to have access to the NIV while doing the daily work.

Each week, there are five daily readings followed by a small group discussion. The daily work will take ten to twenty minutes to complete. In Week One, we will lay some essential groundwork. In Week Two we will begin with Jeremiah's call and continue on through his life chronologically. Along the way, we will become acquainted with the nation of Judah in its final days before the Babylonian captivity. You will also gain some understanding of the covenants, the temple, the law, and the unconditional love of God. You will be blessed to find many similarities between Jeremiah and our Messiah, Jesus Christ, as the study comes to an end.

"It is hard to overstate the significance of the destruction of the Jewish Temple by the Babylonians in 586 BC. Its demolition – the exile of Judah – is perhaps the central calamity of the entire Tanakh (Hebrew Scriptures), even today Judaism grapples with its implications. The prophet of that dark period of Jewish history was Jeremiah, sometimes called the "weeping prophet". In many profound ways Jeremiah prefigured the prophetic ministry of Yeshua (Jesus)". (John J. Parsons, hebrew4christians.com, 2014)

God's words to Jeremiah are as much for us as they were for the people of Jeremiah's day. I am asking God to open your mind and heart to His Truth, and pray that as you study His Word, you will be transformed into the people God has called us to be. I hope you and your small group experience a great time of fellowship over the next seven weeks, and may you come to know our Lord Jesus Christ at a deeper level, through the pages of Jeremiah.

I want to acknowledge those who were a considerable help to me in the preparation of this book: my beloved daughters - Jenette Smith, Anna McCabe and Sandy McDonough, and my close friend and co-worker in the ministry, Fran Maddock. They have been my editors, helping me with ideas, loving suggestions, prayers and support. I thank God for my wonderful husband, Jim, who encouraged me to publish this study and has completed the workbook himself. He had the idea for the book's title, and even drew some of the graphic images in the book! And lastly, I am thankful for my amazing church family – the Christ-followers at Oakwood Community Church who minister the love of Jesus to me on a daily basis!

> *"I will bring him near and he will come close to me, for who is he who will devote himself to be close to me?" declares the Lord. "So you will be my people, and I will be your God." Jeremiah 30:21-22*

WEEK ONE

Understanding the Times

DAY ONE – THE KINGDOM OF ISRAEL

Over the next seven weeks, we are going to look at some amazing events and incredible teaching from God's Word. Always begin with a personal prayer, asking God to reveal His truth to you. The Holy Spirit will be our Teacher as we study the Scriptures together.

Before we open our bibles to the book of Jeremiah, we need to begin with some preparation. A few questions that we will want answered are:

- Who are the people that Jeremiah is speaking to? Is he also speaking to us?
- What does he mean by terms like "covenant", "Judah", "circumcision", "temple"?
- What caused the events that Jeremiah prophesied about?
- What do these events have to do with us?

In order to understand these things, we need to lay some essential groundwork.

History of the Divided Kingdom

After Moses died, Joshua led the people into the land God had promised to Abraham's descendants. (Genesis 15:18-21) They lived for a while being ruled by some special people called "judges".

"Whenever the Lord raised up a judge for them, he was with the judge and saved them out of the hands of their enemies as long as the judge lived; ...but when the judge died, the people returned to ways even more corrupt than those of their fathers, following other gods and serving and worshipping them". Judges 2:18a-19a

But the people wanted a king, so God gave them King Saul - followed by King David, and then his son, King Solomon. Saul first became king of Israel in 1095 BC.

"This is what the Lord, the God of Israel, says: 'I brought Israel up out of Egypt, and I delivered you from the power of Egypt and all the kingdoms that oppressed you.' But you have now rejected your God, who saves you out of all your calamities and distresses. And you have said, 'No, set a king over us.'...finally Saul son of Kish was chosen. Samuel said to all the people, 'Do you see the man the Lord has chosen? There is no one like him among all the people." Then the people shouted, "Long live the king!" 1 Samuel 10:18-19, 21, 24

Up until the end of King Solomon's reign, the country of Israel, the "promised land", was made up of the territory given by God to the twelves tribes or sons of Israel. The name, "Israel" came from Abraham's grandson, Jacob, who had his name changed to "Israel" by God. As the Israelites were freed from slavery in Egypt and miraculously crossed the Red Sea, they entered their new land, previously known as Canaan. Joshua divided the land into portions for each of the sons with a couple of exceptions: Joseph received two parts (one for each of his sons, Ephraim and Manasseh) and Levi did not receive any land, because he was given the priesthood. The sons of Levi were given special towns to live in, as they cared for the tabernacle and the administered the daily sacrifices.

"Now these are the areas the Israelites received as an inheritance in the land of Canaan, which Eleazar the priest, Joshua son of Nun and the heads of the tribal clans of Israel allotted to them. Their inheritances were assigned by lot... as the Lord had commanded through Moses. The Levites

received no share of the land but only towns to live in, with pasturelands for their flocks and herds." Joshua 14:1-2,4

The land of Israel prospered under the reigns of Saul, David and Solomon. But because of the unfortunate lack of wisdom by Solomon's son, Rehoboam, soon after he became king, the kingdom was divided into two parts. Rehoboam remained king over the south, and Jeroboam (not from the lineage of David) became the king of the north. The north was called "Samaria" or "Israel". The south was called, "Judah", but actually included the land that was allotted to two of Jacob's sons - Judah and Benjamin. (See 1 Kings 12:16-20) The split between the north and south happened in 975 BC.

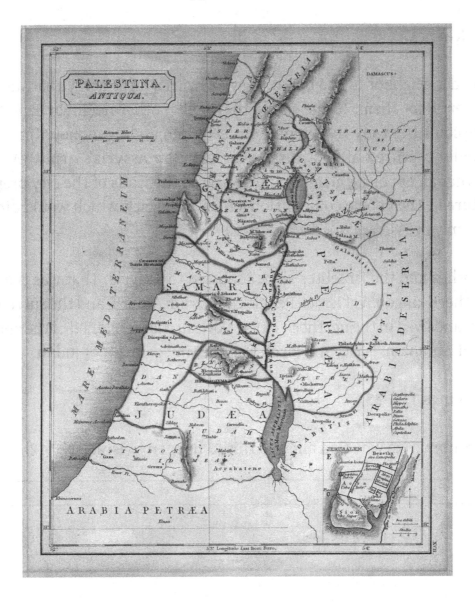

The northern country (Israel) was made up of the land that was allotted to ten of the sons of Jacob. (See Joshua 13:8-19:51). An important thing to note is that Jerusalem (known as the "City of David") and the temple were located in the southern country (Judah). The temple was built by King Solomon. We'll learn more about the temple later.

Now let's fast forward 245 years to 730 BC (about 100 years before Jeremiah). We'll pick up the story when Hoshea was the 20th king of Israel, also called, "Samaria".

<u>The End of the Northern Kingdom</u>

Read 2 Kings 17:1-6

Israel had a neighbor to the north, Assyria, with a large army that was much too powerful for them. To the south, they had another neighbor, Egypt. Both of these countries were threatening Israel by demanding money. King Hoshea was finally captured after a three-year siege by Assyria's army. (A "siege" meant that an opposing army would surround the walls of the city preparing to capture it. The people could no longer leave the city, which would diminish their supply of essential food and water.)

King Hoshea and the Israelites were deported to Assyria. That was the end of the northern kingdom of Israel. People came from Assyria and the surrounding nations, and lived in the northern cities. Now, all that remained of the ancestral family of Abraham, Isaac, and Jacob was the tiny country of Judah.

Read 2 Kings 17:5-23

1. Summarize why God allowed this to happen to Israel. (v.7-12)

   _____

   _____

Read 2 Kings 17:34-41

2. What did God command the Israelites when he made a covenant with them? (v. 35)

_____

_____

The Scofield Bible describes a "covenant" this way:

"The term 'covenant' means a sovereign pronouncement of God (a sacred promise) by which He establishes a relationship of responsibility between
  • Himself and mankind in general
  • Himself and an individual
  • Himself and a nation
  • Himself and a specific human family

The covenants are normally unconditional in the sense that God obligates Himself in grace, by the unrestricted declaration, 'I will' to accomplish certain announced purposes, despite any failure on the part of the person or persons with whom He covenants." (C.I. Scofield, 1917)

The Bible speaks of several covenants that God made with men including:

  • The Edenic Covenant (Gen. 1:28-30, 2:16,17)
  • The Noahic Covenant (Gen. 8:21-9:17)
  • The Abrahamic Covenant (Gen. 12:1-7, 13:14-17, 15:8, 17:1-21)
    ▪ Restated to Isaac and Jacob (Gen. 26:1-5, 28:10-15)
  • The Davidic Covenant (2 Sam. 7:8-16)

All of these covenants were unconditional. God promised to keep them, no strings attached. Man's response to these covenants was to gratefully accept them. Man could do nothing to alter or end a covenant that God had made with man.

Our God is a covenant-keeping God. He had entered into a solemn covenant with the Israelites. The Israelites had broken the covenant. Remember, that the covenants we looked at yesterday were unconditional. Men could do nothing to change those covenants.

But the covenant we are going to look at now is different. The Mosaic Covenant, sometimes called the "Law", was conditional. God said, "If you do this, I will do that". There were specific terms of the covenant spelled out in the books of Exodus, Leviticus, and Deuteronomy. In order for this covenant to be in effect, both parties had to agree to the terms and both had to keep their word. When the New Testament talks about the "Law", it is referring to the terms of the Mosaic Covenant.

Read Exodus 19:1-8

The Israelites had just been delivered from slavery in Egypt. They crossed the Red Sea when God supernaturally parted the waters for them. He told them that He would enter into a very special covenant with them, so that they would be His "treasured possession". God said that he would prosper them in "everything you do", if they would keep His covenant.

In Deuteronomy, Moses gave some details of the terms of the covenant that God made with the people back at Mount Horeb. Moses and the people were about to enter into the "promised land".

Read Deuteronomy 29:1-29

This covenant was a solemn oath, similar to a marriage contract. It was not something to be treated casually.

1. Why did God make this covenant with the Israelites? (v.13)

    _____

    _____

2. God made the covenant both with those who were standing there, and also with (v. 15)

    _____

    _____

3. When a person's heart turns away from the Lord to serve other gods, the Scripture refers to it as a root that produces what? (v. 18)

    _____

    _____

4. In the future when the nations say, "Why has the Lord done this to this land? Why this great outburst of anger? The men will say (v. 25)

    _____

    _____

5. What was the ultimate result of God's anger? (v. 28)

    _____

    _____

Week One: Day Three – Circumcision of the Heart

We who have received salvation through Jesus Christ are true Israelites. We are not Israelites by natural birth, but by spiritual birth. The Holy Spirit has circumcised our hearts, and His message is meant for us as much as it was meant for them.

Read Deuteronomy 30:1-20

1. What does God promise to do if the people return to the Lord and obey Him? (v. 3)

   _____

   _____

Moses prophesies (v.6) that a day is coming when God will perform surgery on people's hearts. He will circumcise their heart and the hearts of their descendants to love the Lord.

Read Romans 2:28-29

2. According to these verses, the work of circumcision is now done in the heart by _____.

3. A circumcised man gets his praise not from men, but from

   _____.

4. Who is a Jew? _____

Read Jeremiah 9:25-26

5. God said He would punish all who are circumcised only _____

   _____.

6. He also said that the whole house of Israel is uncircumcised in _____

   _____.

Read Philippians 3:3 and Romans 9:3-8

7. Who are the true children of God? _____

Read Romans 8:14, 9:25-26, John 1:12-13

If you have received salvation through faith in Christ, then you are an adopted son or daughter of God. You are a spiritual descendant of Abraham. The covenant God made with Abraham and His descendants includes us too. The good news of the Gospel is that by placing our faith in Jesus Christ, He becomes our Righteousness, and all of the requirements of "the Law" have been fulfilled by Christ for us. His blood sacrifice was the punishment you deserved, and He paid the ultimate price for you to be completely justified and sanctified in God's sight. (*For further reading on this read Romans 3:21-24, 4:13-16.*) He was punished for our disobedience – a punishment He didn't deserve - but gladly chose to accept on our behalf. He literally saved our lives.

Reread Deuteronomy 30: 6

This prophecy was fulfilled by Jesus Christ. The circumcision of the heart takes place when anyone – Jew or Gentile – accepts Christ's death as punishment for his own sin, and is forgiven.

"And everyone who calls on the name of the Lord shall be saved." Acts 2:21

Optional: If you have never asked Jesus to be your Lord:

Take the time right now and pray a simple prayer. Humbly and honestly talk to God and tell Him that you believe Jesus died and rose again, and you want to ask Him to be the Lord of your life. You need to ask forgiveness for all you've done wrong in the past (whether intentional or not) and choose to begin to obey God from this day on. Remember – we are all sinners. He promises to wash you with His own blood and cleanse you from all unrighteousness. He will circumcise your heart. Once you place your faith in Christ you will immediately be brought into the kingdom of God, and will be guaranteed a place in eternity with Jesus. What a wonderful promise! Choose life!

"But these are written that you may believe that Jesus is the Messiah, the Son of God, and that by believing you may have life in His name." John 20:31

If you just made the decision to trust in Jesus Christ, then congratulations and welcome to the family of God! It is the best decision you have ever made. You should go back and read this lesson again now.

Make sure to tell someone that you have asked Jesus to be your Lord and Savior.

> *"For it is with your heart that you believe and are justified, and it is with your mouth that you confess your faith and are saved." Romans 10:10*

Week One: Day Four – An Amazing Encounter with God

Today we will read about an encounter that Moses, Joshua and the elders had with an Almighty God. I would say that an encounter like the one you are going to read about is impossible – except that it is described in detail in the book of Exodus. Scripture tells us about the actual agreement between the two parties that would come to be known as "the Old Covenant" or "the Law".

Read Exodus 24:1-18

The events described in Exodus 24 happened back in 1400 BC. In those times, people from different tribes or families, would enter into covenants with each other so that they could help protect each other, help feed and clothe each other, etc. Nations would enter into covenant with other nations to fend off attackers. The Israelites living during that time would have been familiar with what a covenant was. You would keep a covenant, even if you had to give your life to keep it. Entering into a covenant was something that people and tribes took very seriously. Remember, this was at a time in history when keeping your word was expected and the honorable thing to do. People didn't have lawyers - they gave their word and honored their commitment. No one entered into a covenant lightly, they understood that they would be honor-bound to keep every part of it.

Exodus 24 describes the making of the covenant between God and the Israelites.

1. After Moses had shared with the people all of the words of the law and the terms of the covenant, the people responded by saying with one voice, (v.3) "_____".

   _____

2. Moses went up the mountain and saw the God of Israel. Who was with him? (v. 9) _____

   _____

3. What did they do after they saw God? (v.11) _____

   _____

Back then, at the making of a covenant, there was always a solemn covenant meal that the two parties would eat together. It was symbolic, and showed that from that day on they would share everything with each other. They were committed to one another. When Moses, Aaron and the elders ate and drank, they understood that this was a covenant meal – representing a new partnership with God. The seventy elders were representatives of all of the people.

Read Exodus 25:1-22

God gave instructions to Moses regarding building a sanctuary for worship. This sanctuary, or tabernacle, would have to be easily transported, since they were still in the wilderness. Eventually the design of the sanctuary would become a permanent structure (the temple) in Jerusalem.

Inside the tabernacle would be some furniture which God Himself would design. He began with the ark.

The ark was a wooden box with a lid that opened so that items could be stored inside. The box was made of acacia wood and overlaid with pure gold inside and out. The ark could be easily transported by two poles that would slip thru rings fastened to the ark. The poles were also overlaid with pure gold.

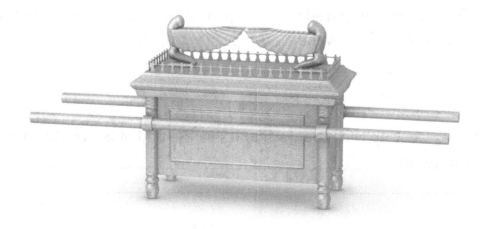

4. Where would God specifically meet with the people? (v. 21)

_____

_____

Inside the ark, Moses would keep the "Words of the Covenant", also called "the Testimony", which were the two stone tablets written by the hand of God. This was the holy document representing the covenant that they had witnessed and agreed to. The Ark of the Covenant was kept in the Holy of Holies – highlighting the great value of the covenant relationship God had with the Israelites.

The cover on top of the ark formed a seat or bench. It was called the "mercy seat" sometimes called the "atonement cover". On the mercy seat were two carved angels, or cherubim, with wings attached. The angels were a reminder that this ark was holy, and that God's Presence was there. Everything was overlaid in pure gold. (Exodus 37:1-9)

God told Moses that He Himself would meet with the people over the mercy seat between the wings of the cherubim. He said His holy Presence would be found there. The Ark of the Covenant was so holy that no one dared touch it or he would die. (Exodus 40:34-35)

Once the tabernacle was completed, the Ark of the Covenant was placed inside the inner room, called the "Holy of Holies" or "Most Holy Place". It was shielded behind a thick veil. No one, not even the priests, were allowed to go inside the Most Holy Place. Only once a year, the high priest could go inside, but even then the people were afraid that he might die in the Presence of God – so they tied a rope to his ankle when he went in. (To study all of the furniture in the tabernacle, the sacrifices, the priesthood, and festivals, read Exodus 25-40).

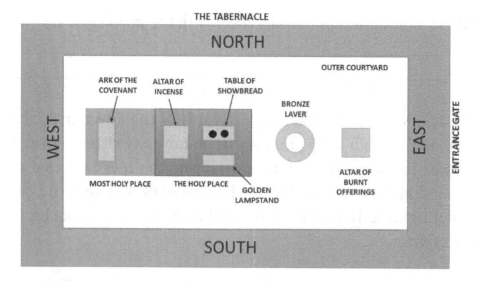

400 years later when David became king, he wanted to build God a permanent dwelling – a home for the Ark of the Covenant. God agreed to a permanent sanctuary in Jerusalem. But God said that David's son, Solomon, would be the one to build the temple because David had been in battles and had blood on his hands. God gave David specific details on how to build it.

Read 1 Kings 6:11-22

So Solomon built the permanent temple in Jerusalem. This temple was the center of Jewish life from the time it was built and dedicated in 957 BC., until the day it was destroyed in 586 BC.

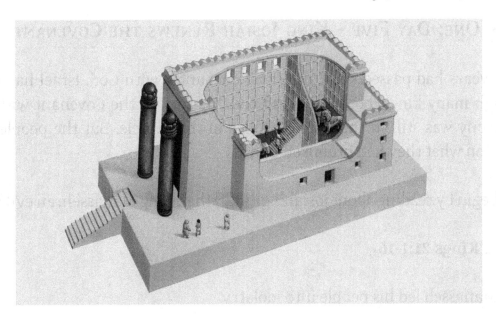

5. Based on today's readings, how important was the Mosaic Covenant to the people of Israel?

_____

_____

Many years had passed since that first encounter with God. Israel had been through many kings, both good and bad. The Ark of the Covenant with the Testimony was still in the Holy of Holies in the Temple. But the people had forgotten what they had promised God.

Let's begin by reading about Josiah's grandfather, King Manasseh, an evil king.

Read 2 Kings 21:1-16

King Manasseh led his people into idolatry.

1. What were some of the practices of Manasseh that we are told about in 2 Kings? (v. 3-6)

    _____

    _____

Read 2 Kings 22:1-11

King Josiah was only eight years old when he began to reign. Jeremiah was close in age, most likely a few years younger than Josiah. When King Josiah was twenty-six years old, he discovered the Book of the Law - including the first five books of the Bible called "the Pentateuch". Since the Scripture describes this as a discovery, it seems likely that the Book of the Law had not been read during the fifty-five year reign of his grandfather King Manasseh, or the two-year reign of Josiah's father, King Amon.

2. What did King Josiah do when he heard the words of the Book of the Law? (v. 11)

    _____

    _____

Read 2 Kings 23:1-3

3. What did King Josiah vow to do by renewing the covenant? (v.3)

_____

_____

4. After the people heard the words of the Law, how did they respond? (v. 3)

_____

_____

This revival happened in the 18th year of King Josiah. Jeremiah began his public ministry in the 13th year of Josiah. So Jeremiah must have witnessed this great revival and renewing of the covenant.

Unfortunately, the people of Judah under the reign of the previous kings had been so deeply entrenched in idolatry, that they fell right back into their bad habits as soon as Josiah died.

Congratulations! You are done with the background preparations. As we begin our study of the book of Jeremiah, I pray that you will be encouraged and inspired by God's prophet, and will grow stronger in your faith each day.

WEEK ONE SMALL GROUP DISCUSSION –
Good Kings, Bad Kings

Open in prayer.

Study the chart below to become familiar with the general timeline of the kings. (Locate Jeremiah, Moses and Joshua, the Divided Monarchy, the Fall of Samaria and the destruction of the temple.)

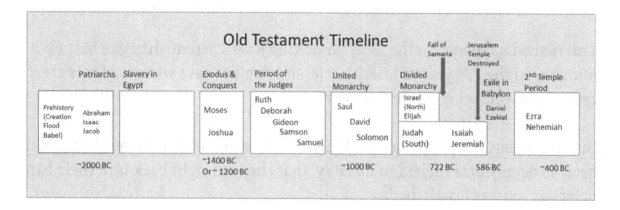

1. If this is the first time you have studied Old Testament history, you may not have seen a timeline like this before. Maybe you've heard bible stories as a child, but never knew how the stories fit into the timeline of history. What information is new to you?

   _____

   _____

2. When did these events that you read about during the past week occur on this timeline?
   • the Covenant made between Moses and God_____
   • Solomon built the temple_____
   • The monarchy was divided_____
   • The North (Israel or Samaria) fell _____
   • The South (Judah) fell and the people went into Exile_____

Study carefully the kings of Judah to find out who the good kings were, who the evil kings were, and who led revivals. Notice the last five kings, who reigned during the life of Jeremiah.

972 BC	King	Evil	Good	Revival
	Rehobohoam	X		
	Abijah	X		
	Asa		X	
	Jehoshaphat			X
	Jehoram	X		
	Ahaziah	X		
	Athaliah	X		
	Joash			X
	Amaziah		X	
	Uzziah		X	
	Jotham		X	
	Ahaz	X		
	Hezekiah			X
	Manasseh	X		
	Amon	X		
	Josiah			X
	Johahaz	X		
	Jehoiakim	X		
	Jehoiachin	X		
598 BC	Zedekiah	X		

As a group, look up each of these kings below in 2 Chronicles and read a brief summary of his reign. The last five kings – from Josiah to Zedekiah - we will be covering later in detail, so we won't read about them now.

Rehoboam – 2 Chron. 12:13-14
Abijah – 2 Chron. 13:1-2, 21
Asa – 2 Chron. 14:1-6, 15:17-19, 16:12-14
Jehoshaphat – 2 Chron. 17:1-6, 20:30-33
Jehoram – 2 Chron. 21:1-7, 12-19
Ahaziah – 2 Chron. 22:1-4, 9-12
Athaliah – 2 Chron. 23:11-15
Joash – 2 Chron. 24:1-4, 25
Amaziah – 2 Chron. 25:1-2, 25-28
Uzziah – 2 Chron. 26:1-5, 21-23
Jotham – 2 Chron. 27:1-2, 6-9

Ahaz – 2 Chron. 28:1-5, 22-25
Hezekiah – 2 Chron. 29:1-6, 27-30; 32:30-32
Manasseh – 2 Chron. 33:1-7, 19-20
Amon – 2 Chron. 33:21-24

3. What did the good kings do that qualified them to be labeled as "good"?
   _____
   _____

4. What did the evil kings do that caused them to be labeled "evil"?
   _____
   _____

5. What did the "revival kings" do to be given their own special category?
   _____
   _____

The Mosaic Covenant

6. Discuss what you remember about the Mosaic Covenant from your daily readings.
   - Where was the location of the original covenant made?
   - Who were the people involved?
   - What did they do to seal the covenant?
   - What were the terms of the Covenant?

7. Were the terms of the covenant clear enough for the people to understand?

8. Why do you think the people agreed to keep these extremely difficult terms? Do you think that the people thought they could keep these terms?

9. Do you think God knew the people would not be able to keep the terms of the covenant? If so, what was His purpose? (Read Romans 3:19-20, 8:3-4, 10:1-4)

10. Many people today think that they are keeping the Law and are good enough to go to heaven on their own merits. Do you think more people would decide to follow Christ if they understood what He has done for them? How can the church help people understand that we are saved by God's grace and not by our own works? (Ephesians 2:8-9)

11. What did you learn this past week that will help you better understand the times Jeremiah lived in?

As you close your small group discussion for Week One, take some time to pray for one another, praying that each member of the group will be encouraged and strengthened as you work through this study together.

WEEK TWO

Jeremiah's Early Years –
King Josiah's Reign

Day One – The Call

To understand the story of Jeremiah, it's important to remember that the people had agreed and entered into a solemn covenant with God saying, "Everything He has said, we will do". Almost immediately after this pledge, they disobeyed God and the terms of the covenant, by worshipping the gods of the foreign nations around them. As a result of their disobedience, the people living in the northern kingdom (Israel) were captured and forced to leave their land, just like the terms of the covenant had described. This happened in 722 BC.

Now the kingdom of Judah was all that was left of God's covenant people. The kings of Judah had been a mixture of both good and bad (see the Small Group discussion Week One). The people, however, continued to worship the gods of the surrounding nations.

The book of Jeremiah begins in 626 BC. Josiah was the king. Babylon was becoming more powerful in the north, although Nebuchadnezzar had not yet taken the throne of his father. Egypt was also gaining strength in the south. Little Judah was sandwiched between these two powerful nations.

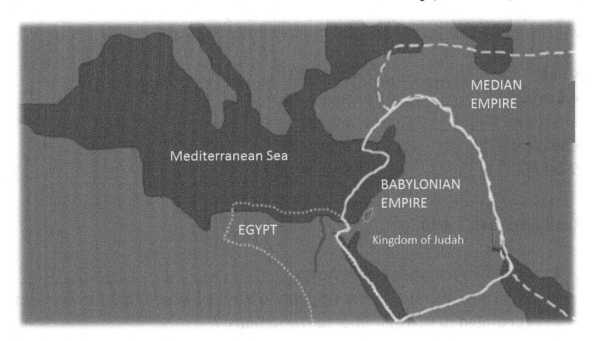

Solomon's temple in Jerusalem was still the center of life for the Jews. The Ark of the Covenant remained in the temple, inside the Holy of Holies (or the "Most Holy Place"), behind the veil.

Read Jeremiah 1:1-3

Jeremiah's father was Hilkiah the priest. (He is not the high priest mentioned in 2 Kings 22:8, but was of the family of priests that lived in Anathoth. See Joshua 21:1-3, 17-19). Anathoth was three miles north of Jerusalem. This is where Jeremiah lived with his family when he first received the call from God.

> "Anathoth is a priestly city within the lands of the tribe of Benjamin, on the border between Judah and Israel. It pledges allegiance to neither kingdom. The priests of Anathoth are not active in the Jerusalem Temple; rather, they live quiet lives, tilling their fields." (Jeremiah: the Fate of a Prophet, B. Lau, 2013, p. 15)

Jeremiah was called by God during the 13th year of King Josiah's reign. Remember, Josiah was only eight years old when he became king because his father, King Amon, was murdered. Now the king was the ripe old age of twenty-one. Jeremiah was in his teens, just slightly younger than the king.

List the <u>number of years</u> each of these five kings reigned:

Josiah   _____ (2 Kings 22:1)
Jehoahaz   _____ (2 Kings 23:31)
Jehoiakim   _____ (2 Kings 23:36)
Jehoiachin   _____ (2 Kings 24:8)
Zedekiah   _____ (2 Kings 24:18)

Read Jeremiah 1:4-10

1. God knew Jeremiah before he was _____.
2. What was Jeremiah's first response when he learned that he had been appointed to be a "prophet to the nations"?

   _____
   _____

3. What was God's answer to Jeremiah?

   _____
   _____

God appointed Jeremiah to the high calling of a prophet. Jeremiah would speak the words that God Himself would put in his mouth. But Jeremiah would not just be a local prophet, speaking to the people in his hometown or in Judah. God would also use him to speak to the surrounding nations, and the world. God told Jeremiah that He would always be with him, and that He would deliver him from his enemies. Jeremiah had nothing to be afraid of. God would protect him.

Let's compare Jeremiah's call with another call of God – this time in the New Testament.

Read Matthew 28:18-20, John 15:16

4. Who in the New Testament was also told to speak to the nations as God's messengers? _____

   _____

5. What did God promise them? (Matthew 28:20)

    _____

    _____

> *"In him we were also chosen, having been predestined according to the plan of him who works out everything in conformity with the purpose of his will, in order that we, who were the first to hope in Christ, might be for the praise of his glory." Ephesians 1:11-12*

6. Paul, speaking to the church at Ephesus, said that we were also chosen. How is Jeremiah's call similar to the calling we have all received by God?

    _____

    _____

Read Jeremiah 1:11-19

Jeremiah had just learned that he had been chosen and appointed to be a prophet of God. Jeremiah complained, "Ah, Sovereign Lord, I don't know how to speak. I am only a child!" In other words, "No thanks! Get someone else!"

But God responded by telling him, "Do not say, I am only a child. You must go to everyone I send you to and say whatever I command you. Do not be afraid of them for I am with you and will rescue you." (Jeremiah 1:6-8)

Then the Lord gave him two visual images that would help him understand why it was important that he bring God's message to the people.

1.   What was the first image Jeremiah saw? (v. 11)

_____

_____

The meaning of the almond tree branch is very significant. The word, "almond tree" in Hebrew is "shaqed". It is almost the same as the word, "shoqed" which means to be awake, watch, or be alert. God said, "You have seen correctly for I am **watching** to see that my word is fulfilled" (v. 12). The almond tree and the concept of watching are tied closely together.

The almond tree produces its fruit in the spring earlier than any other fruit-bearing tree. In the kingdoms of Judah and Israel, the almond had become a symbol of promise and quickness – due to its early flowering. This would have been familiar to the people because almond trees were plentiful.

Some other uses of the almond tree:

- Back in Moses's day, Aaron's rod - a dead branch - brought forth almond flowers. (Num. 17:8)
- The menorah (one of the items in the Temple) was a large candlestick that was designed according to God's instructions. It had three cups on each side shaped like almond blossoms. On the center trunk of the candlestick there were four cups shaped like almond blossoms. (Exodus 37:17-22)

- The Jews ate almonds at their New Year celebration – the traditional beginning of spring.

Almonds symbolize the beauty of new life, the first or earliest buds to appear on a branch after the dead season of winter was over.

There is symbolic meaning in both the almond and the dead branch of the almond tree. Just like Aaron's dead branch that budded, Jesus Christ rose from the dead as the first of many who will also rise at the Resurrection of the Dead. He is called, "the Righteous Branch".

> *"In that day the Branch of the Lord will be beautiful and glorious..."* (Isaiah 4:2)

> *"A shoot will come up from the stump of Jesse; from his roots a Branch will bear fruit. The Spirit of the Lord will rest on him..."* (Isaiah 11:1-2)

The candlestick (menorah) in the temple was also symbolic of Christ – who is the Light of the world. The fact that the menorah is designed like the "almond tree branch" was important. It meant that God would quickly supply new life and light to a dark world.

Jeremiah would have understood by this vision that God was "watching over" his people to perform his Word, and that they could trust him to act quickly to bring life back from the dead.

2. What was the second image? (v. 13)

_____

_____

The boiling pot represented the turmoil facing Judah on all sides. God was revealing the future to Jeremiah. He said that the enemy would come from the north (indicated by the pot tilting toward the south in their direction). The enemy would be a coalition of several kings. All of the towns in Judah including Jerusalem would be affected – no one would be safe from these enemies.

These judgments were coming from God because of their wickedness: (v. 16)

- They forsook God
- They burned incense to other gods
- They worshipped what their hands had made

3. What did God promise Jeremiah? (v.19)

_____

_____

Jesus said something similar the night He was betrayed.

"I have told you these things so that in me you may have peace. In this world you will have trouble. But take heart! I have overcome the world." (John 16:33)

Read Jeremiah Chapter 13:1-11

It's an understatement to say that Jeremiah was given some unusual assignments! God was making His message clear, by demonstrating with visual images. Use the NIV version to fill in the blanks.

1. "For as a belt is bound around a man's waist, so I bound the _____ house of _____ to me and the whole house of _____ to me, declares the Lord, "to be _____ people for my _____ and _____ and _____. But they have not listened." (v.11)

God was faithful to the covenant He had entered into with Israel. The Jews seemed to have forgotten their covenant with God.

2. God said that the people: (v. 10)
    *   Refuse to _____ to my words
    *   Follow the stubbornness of their _____
    *   Go after other _____ to serve and worship them

3. And so these people (just like Jeremiah's belt) will be completely _____. (v. 10)

Read Jeremiah 3:6-15

God viewed the covenant with Israel much like a marriage contract. He said that Israel and her sister Judah, had been unfaithful and had committed adultery by worshipping other gods.

Let's look at a passage In the New Testament speaking to Christ's followers.

Read Ephesians 1:11-14

4. What is God's ultimate purpose for those of us who hope in Christ? (v.12)

_____

_____

The image of Jeremiah's linen belt holds special meaning to each of us who have been saved through faith in Jesus Christ. As God's chosen people, we have as our purpose: to bring praise and glory to our Savior. Let us not be like those that God considered "useless" as a rotten belt.

5. What do you consider your purpose in life? Is it different from God's purpose for you? Why or why not?

_____

_____

Read Jeremiah 12:1-4

Jeremiah had a question for God. He said he wanted to discuss the matter of justice.

6. In your own words, what is the question Jeremiah is asking God?

_____

_____

Read Jeremiah 12:5-6

Jeremiah received a response from God, but God doesn't give him the answer he was looking for. God began by saying that things were going to get much worse – not better - and he should prepare himself. God said that Jeremiah was going to have to learn to "run with horses". He would have to walk in difficult places. Even his family would deal treacherously with him. Not exactly the message that Jeremiah hoped to hear!

Read Jeremiah 15:10-21

How did Jeremiah feel about speaking a message of "coming disaster" to the people? This passage gives us some insight into how difficult it was for this prophet.

7. Why does Jeremiah wish his mother had not given him birth? (v.10)

_____

_____

8. What brought Jeremiah joy and delight?(v.16)

_____

_____

9. Who did Jeremiah never sit with? (v.17)

_____

_____

10. Why did he sit alone? (v.17)

_____

_____

11. What was God's response to Jeremiah's self-pity? (v.19)

_____

_____

12. What were God's promises to Jeremiah in verses 20-21?
    • I will make you_____ to this people.
    • I am with you _____and save you.
    • I will save you from the hands of the wicked and _____ _____from the grasp of the cruel.

Paul the Apostle also had more than his share of difficulty. Paul wrote to the Corinthians:

"But we have this treasure in jars of clay to show this all-surpassing power is from God and not from us. We are hard-pressed on every side, but not crushed; perplexed but not in despair; persecuted, but not abandoned; struck down, but not destroyed...for we who are alive are always being given over to death for Jesus' sake, so that his life may also be revealed in our mortal body." 2 Corinthians 4:7-9

Jesus never said life would be easy. But He did say He would be with us through it all. And that any suffering we endure for His sake would reap eternal rewards.

"For your sake we face death all day long; we are considered as sheep to be slaughtered. No in all these things we are more than conquerors through him who loved us." Romans 8:36-37

Week Two: Day Four – God's Instructions

Read Jeremiah 16:1-18

Today's reading gives some specific instructions that God gave to his prophet. God expected Jeremiah to act differently than other people. Jeremiah was to set an example by his life and his behavior. It seemed that God was training Jeremiah, and was teaching him how to respond when the people would reject both him and God's message.

Here are three specific instructions that God gave to Jeremiah regarding his own behavior:

1. You must not _____ or have _____ and _____ in this place. (v. 2)
2. Do not enter a house where there is a _____; do not go to mourn or show _____.(v. 5)
3. And do not enter a house where there is _____ and sit down to eat and drink. (v.8)

Then God informed Jeremiah that the people would not understand why bad things were happening to them. He told Jeremiah that they will ask him questions, and this is how God wanted him to answer.

4. When the people ask, "Why has the Lord decreed such disaster? What wrong have we done?" (v. 10-12) He should answer:
   - Your fathers _____ me
   - And followed other _____
   - And served and _____ them
   - But you have behaved _____ than your fathers.
5. What reason did God give Jeremiah for telling him not to marry and have children? (v.4)

   _____

   _____

6. What reason did God give for not wanting Jeremiah to attend funerals? (v.5-7)

_____

_____

7. Why should Jeremiah not participate in the feasts? (v.9)

_____

_____

8. Do you believe that we (Christ's followers) are called to separate ourselves from worldly celebrations? Why or why not?

_____

_____

9. In what ways have you separated yourself from the world? Can the unbelievers who know you, tell that you are a Christian?

_____

_____

"Do not love the world or anything in the world. If anyone loves the world, the love of the Father is not in him." 1 John 2:15

"You adulterous people, don't you know that friendship with the world is hatred toward God? Anyone who chooses to be a friend of the world becomes an enemy of God." James 4:4

God goes on to say that in the future, people will stop talking about how God delivered His people out of Egypt and led them into the "promised land" of Israel. They will begin to talk about a second deliverance. This time God will deliver His people out of the land of the north – Babylon and Assyria.

10. What is God's promise in Jeremiah 16:15?

_____

_____

God said that even though the people had followed the inclinations of their evil hearts, that He would still bring them back and restore them to the land that He had given to Abraham, Isaac, and Jacob. God wanted them to have hope. They could trust in God's faithfulness. God's people should always hope.

Hope for Christians

In 1 Corinthians 13 while describing godly love, we learn that hope is a characteristic of love.

> *"It (love) always protects, always trusts, always **hopes**, always perseveres.... And now these three remain: faith, **hope** and love." 1 Corinthians 13:7, 13*

God always provides His people with a message of hope. In the New Testament, we are told to hope that the Lord Jesus Christ will return one day for his people. Paul wrote to the church in Thessalonica,

> *"Brothers, we do not want you to be ignorant about those who fall asleep, or to grieve like the rest of men, who have no **hope**. We believe that Jesus died and rose again and so we believe that God will bring with Jesus those who have fallen asleep in him...For the Lord himself will come down from heaven, with a loud command, with the voice of the archangel and with the trumpet call of God, and the dead in Christ will rise first. After that, we who are still alive and are left will be caught up together with them in the clouds to meet the Lord in the air. And so we will be with the Lord forever." 1 Thessalonians 4:13-14, 16-17*

> *"To him who overcomes I will give the right to sit with me on my throne, just as I overcame and sat down with my Father on his throne." Revelation 3:21*

> *"For in this hope we were saved. But hope that is seen is no hope at all. Who hopes for what he already has?" Romans 8:24*

"Everything that was written in the past was written to teach us, so that through endurance and the encouragement of the Scriptures we might have hope." Romans 15:4

11. Do you have hope today? If so, describe what you hope for?

_____

_____

Read Jeremiah 18:1-12

Once again, God instructed Jeremiah to do something that would illustrate His message. This time He used clay, a potter's wheel, and a potter. Jeremiah was told to go down to the potter's house and when he got there, he found the potter working at the wheel.

1. What was wrong with the pot that the potter was working on? (v.4)

   _____

   _____

2. What did the potter do as a result? _____

   _____

3. In God's illustration, God is the potter. Who does the clay represent?

   _____ (v. 6)

4. What does God reserve the right to do? (v. 8-10)

   _____

   _____

5. God told Judah in verse 11 that He had prepared disaster for them. They needed to turn from their evil ways. What is their response?

_____

_____

Paul the Apostle used this illustration from Jeremiah in his letter to the Romans.

> *"But who are you, O man, to talk back to God? 'Shall what is formed say to him who formed it, 'Why did you make me like this?' Does not the potter have the right to make out of the same lump of clay some pottery for noble purposes and some for common use?" Romans 9:20-21*

The "potter and the clay" speaks of the sovereignty of Almighty God. Since God created us, and since He owns everything, and holds all power, do we really have the right to question His fairness?

God - who knows all things, has all power, and is eternal - obviously thinks differently than men do. What we consider a success is quite different from what God considers a success. For example, God says a man is rich if he is full of love and if he's been forgiven of all his sins. It has nothing to do with money.

Jesus, born in a cave with animals and laid in a manger for a bed, never owned material things. Man would consider Jesus very poor. Yet by God's standards, Jesus was a very rich man – rich in holiness, goodness, righteousness, love, joy, peace, humility, mercy, etc. God places higher value on invisible things, spiritual things, things that we carry inside our heart. He knows that all material things will perish – but the invisible virtues that we carry in our heart will last forever. They will go with us when we cross into eternity.

> *"So we fix our eyes not on what is seen, but on what is unseen. For what is seen is temporary, but what is unseen is eternal." 2 Corinthians 4:18*

6. Do you ever think like the clay in the illustration, "why did you make me like this?" Do you ever struggle with the issue of fairness with God?

_____

_____

7. Think back over your entire life. Has God treated you fairly?

    _____

    _____

The world's value system is very different than God's. That's why it is important once we become Christians, that we begin to read God's Word, and start the process of conforming to God's value system. Thankfully, the Holy Spirit is at work in each of us, revealing truth and teaching us God's ways. Although we were saved and forgiven (justified) the moment we believed, the transformation of being made holy will take time. It is possible to speed up the process though, through time spent with Jesus – in prayer, in worship, and in His Word.

The Earthenware Jar

Read Jeremiah 19:1-6, 10-15

The Lord told Jeremiah to go and buy a clay jar from a potter. He took along some of the elders and priests and went out to the Valley of Ben Hinnom, in the city of Topheth.

8. The name of the city of Topheth will be changed to the Valley of (v.6)

    _____

    _____

While these people were watching, Jeremiah was instructed to break the jar for the second part of his message.

9. The nation and the city of Topheth will be (v.11) _____, and cannot be _____.

Then Jeremiah returned from his trip to the Valley of Ben Hinnom.

10. Where did Jeremiah go stand and speak next? (v.14)

    _____

    _____

11. Who did he speak to?_____

_____

12. God said that disaster was pronounced against them because they were
_____ _____and would

not _____

Read Jeremiah 6:10

Did you know that it is possible to close our ears to the truth? We can refuse to listen if we find that what is being said offends us. We must decide that we will open our ears to hear what the Spirit is saying. God will speak to us through His word, through other believers, through prayer, and through our circumstances.

> *"He who belongs to God **hears** what God says." John 8:47*

> *"The watchman opens the gate for him, and the sheep **listen** to his voice. He calls his own sheep by name and leads them out. When he has brought out all his own, he goes on ahead of them, and his sheep follow him because they know his voice." John 10:3, 4*

> *"Blessed is the one who reads the words of this prophecy, and blessed are those who **hear** it and take to heart what is written in it, because the time is near." Revelation 1:3*

> *"He who has an ear, let him **hear** what the Spirit says to the churches." Revelation 2:7*

God is continually speaking to us. Spend some quiet time now in prayer, listening for God's voice.

WEEK TWO SMALL GROUP DISCUSSION –
THE FINAL FIVE!

(Josiah, Jehoahaz, Jehoiakim, Jehoiachin, and Zedekiah)

Open in prayer.

Review Questions:

1. What have you learned about Jeremiah the prophet?
    *   Describe what you've learned about his personal life
    *   Describe what you know about His relationship with God
    *   Describe what you have seen so far about His relationship with the people

2. (Look back briefly through Week Two) What do you remember about the specific messages that Jeremiah spoke to the people?
3. What teachings have you heard from Jeremiah that can also be found in the New Testament?
4. Have you been able to apply any of this week's lessons to your own life? If so, describe how.

Read 2 Kings 23:29-30 – King Josiah

In this Scripture passage, we learn how King Josiah died. It must have been a very sad day for Jeremiah. Josiah had been Jeremiah's king since he was a young boy.

1. Describe the events that led to King Josiah's death. (see 2 Chronicles 35:20-27 for more details)
2. As a group, name some of the highlights of King Josiah's life (from Week One – Day Five). (1 Kings 22 and 23)
3. On what battle field was King Josiah killed? What famous battle will take place there in the future? (Revelation 16:14,16) (Megiddo and Armageddon are the same place)

When King Josiah died, his son, Jehoahaz (also known as "Shallum") was made king. He was twenty-three years old. He only reigned for three months, but he did evil during those three months. The year was 609 BC.

Read 2 Kings 23:31-34 – King Jehoahaz

1. Describe the events that brought to an end King Jehoahaz's reign.
2. Was it Babylon, Assyria or Egypt that took King Jehoahaz prisoner?
3. Where did Jehoahaz die?

Read Jeremiah 22:10-12

4. Did this prophecy by Jeremiah prove to be true? Did Jehoahaz ever return to Judah? _____

Read 2 Kings 23:35-24:6 – King Jehoiakim

Next, came King Jehoiakim (also known as Eliakim), another son of Josiah. Notice that Jehoiakim was twenty-five when he started to reign –his brother, Jehoahaz, was twenty-three years old. So the crown rightfully should have belonged to Jehoiakim in the first place. He reigned from 609 BC to 597 BC.

The <u>1st deportation</u> **took place in 605 BC** during King Jehoiakim's reign. Nebuchadnezzar invaded the land, and took back with him young Daniel and his friends, some officials, and some articles from the temple. (See Daniel 1:1-7)

1. Who made Jehoahaz king? (2 Kings 23:30)
2. How long did King Jehoiakim reign?
3. What king invaded the land during his reign? (2 Kings 24:1)
4. What king did Jehoiakim pay a tribute of silver and gold to, and taxed the land to raise the money? (2 Kings 23:35)
5. Why didn't the king of Egypt march out again from his own country? (2 Kings 24:7)

Read Jeremiah 22:13-23

6. Where did Jehoiakim die?
7. Describe Jehoiakim's funeral.

Read 2 Kings 24:6-16 and 25:27-30 – King Jehoiachin

Next, was Jehoiachin, who was only eighteen years old when he became the king. He was the son of Jehoiakim. The 2<u>nd</u> deportation happened only 3 months into Jehoiachin's reign. The year was 597 BC.

1. How long did Jehoiachin reign? (2 Kings 24:8)
2. During the deportation of King Jehoiachin, describe what was carried into exile in Babylon. (2 Kings 24:10-16)
3. What happened to Jehoiachin while he was in Babylon? Did he ever return to Israel? (2 Kings 25:27-30)

Read Jeremiah 22:24-30

4. What happened to Jehoiachin's offspring? (v.30)

Read 2 Kings 24:18-25:21 – King Zedekiah

Finally, there was King Zedekiah (also called, "Mattaniah"). Zedekiah was Jehoiachin's uncle and the third and last son of Josiah. He reigned from 597 BC to 586 BC.

The **3<u>rd</u> deportation took place in the 11ᵗʰ year of King Zedekiah's reign. The year was 586 BC.** In the 3ʳᵈ and final deportation, the Babylonian army set fire to the entire city, the temple, the palace, and the surrounding cities. Anything of value was carried off to Babylon at that time.

1. How long did Zedekiah reign? (2 Kings 24:18)
2. Describe the events that led to Zedekiah's capture? (2 Kings 25:1-5)

3. What happened to Zedekiah and his sons when they were captured? (2 Kings 25:6-7)
4. What was taken in the deportation to Babylon? (2 Kings 25:11-17)
5. What happened to the temple, the palace, the walls around the city of Jerusalem, etc.?(2 Kings 25:9-10)
6. What happened to the chief priest, the temple doorkeepers, the other officers and royal advisers? (2 Kings 25:18-21)
7. How many total deportations were there?
8. Review what was deported at each deportation, and what king was in power during each.
9. What was the date of the final deportation?

As you end your small group discussion for Week Two, take time to pray for one another, encouraging and strengthening each other.

WEEK THREE

Jehoiakim's Reign

DAY ONE – DEATH SENTENCE!

You will be reading in chapter 26 today, then back to chapter 20 tomorrow. Remember that Jeremiah's messages are not in chronological order.

Read Jeremiah 26:1-19

King Jehoiakim was on the throne. His father Josiah was dead. His younger brother, Jehoahaz has been captured and taken to Egypt where he died. The year was 609 BC. Nebuchadnezzar had not yet come to power in Babylon.

Jeremiah had been commanded by God to go and stand in the courtyard of the Lord's House and speak to the people who have come there to worship.

1. What does God say will happen if they turn from their evil ways? (v. 3)

    _____

    _____

2. How did the priests and prophets respond to God's message? (v. 11)

    _____

    _____

Jeremiah again spoke to the officials and people. He added, "If you put me to death, you will bring the guilt of innocent blood on yourselves and on this city and on those who live in it."

3. What did the officials and the people tell the priests and the (false) prophets? (v.16)

_____

_____

The elders stepped forward and reminded the people of another occasion where a prophet gave similar warnings.

4. Who was the other prophet?

_____

_____

5. What king was on the throne at that time?

_____

_____

6. How did the elders respond? (v. 19)

_____

_____

Jeremiah was speaking in the courtyard of the Lord's house. Most likely he was standing in the Court of the Gentiles – the largest area inside the wall. Those who were circumcised were allowed to go further inside the inner courts, but Jeremiah wanted all of the people to hear God's message. Circumcised men could go further past the Court of Women, but only as far as the Court of the Israelites. The priests could go all the way into the Holy Place. (Numbers 18:2,3, 22-23) But no one went into the Most Holy Place -only the High Priest on the Day of Atonement – no exceptions. (Leviticus 16)

The people knew that the animal sacrifices would temporarily forgive their sin, but none of their sacrifices would ever give them access into the Most

Holy Place – the Presence of God. Nothing they could do would make them holy enough to enter the Most Holy Place. As if to remind them of the barrier between them and God, there was a thick veil in front of the Ark of the Covenant.

Read Jeremiah 11:18-23

God revealed to Jeremiah that the men of his hometown of Anathoth were plotting against him. He realized that he had been led like a lamb to the slaughter. He asked God to judge between him and his enemies. He committed his cause to God, and put his entire defense in God's hands.

There was another man in the Bible who was led like a lamb to the slaughter.

Read John 7:25-31, 40-52

7. What were the Jewish leaders arguing about? (v.43)

    _____

    _____

Isaiah's prophecy was referring to Jesus Christ, the Lamb of God. John the Baptist saw Jesus walking toward him and said, *"Look, the Lamb of God, who takes away the sin of the world".* John 1:29

Jesus stood before the assembly on the day he would be crucified.

> *"Herod plied him with many questions, but Jesus gave him no answer. The chief priests and the teachers of the law were standing there, vehemently accusing him." Luke 23:9-10*

Read Isaiah 53:7-9

Jesus knew that he was being led like a lamb to the slaughter. But that was the very reason that He had come. He came to offer himself as a sacrifice for sin. When the perfect Lamb of God shed His sinless blood and died for the sins of the world, the veil in the temple was torn, finally giving mankind access to the

Presence of God in all of His holiness. The illustration of the torn veil couldn't have been made any clearer to those who knew the Mosaic Covenant. At the exact moment that Jesus took his last breath, the veil was torn completely in two.

> *"And when Jesus had cried out again in a loud voice, he gave up his spirit. At that moment the curtain of the temple was torn in two from top to bottom. The earth shook and the rocks split." Matthew 27:50-51*

Read Jeremiah 20:1-6

Pashur was a priest, and a chief officer in the Temple. Before he had Jeremiah put in stocks overnight at the Upper Gate to the Temple, he first had him beaten. What was Jeremiah's crime? He was speaking the truth to the people – telling them to stop sinning and turn to God. For this he was being punished.

Jesus told us that following Him would be costly. He told us that there would be persecution.

> *"Blessed are those who are persecuted because of righteousness, for theirs is the kingdom of heaven. Blessed are you when people insult you, persecute you and falsely say all kinds of evil against you because of me. Rejoice and be glad, because great is your reward in heaven, for in the same way they persecuted the prophets who were before you." Matthew 5:10-12*

Let's remember what Paul the apostle suffered for the sake of the Gospel:

"in great endurance; in troubles, hardships and distresses; in beatings, imprisonments and riots; in hard work, sleepless nights and hunger; ...through glory and dishonor, bad report and good report; genuine, yet regarded as impostors; known yet regarded as unknown; dying, and yet we live on; beaten, and yet not killed; sorrowful, yet always rejoicing; poor, yet making many rich; having nothing yet possessing everything."
2 Corinthians 6:4b-5, 8-10

We may have to endure persecution, but we can find comfort in these words:

"Our light and momentary troubles are achieving for us an eternal glory that far outweighs them all. So we fix our eyes not on what is seen but on what is unseen. For what is seen is temporary, but what is unseen is eternal." 2 Corinthians 4:17-18

Consider what Jeremiah prophesied to Pashur after he was removed from the stocks.

1. The Lord's name for you is (Jer. 20:3) _____ - _____ which means "terror on every side".
2. I will make you a (v.4) _____ to yourself and all your friends.
3. With your own eyes you will see them (v.4) _____.
4. I will hand all Judah over to _____.
5. I will also hand over to their enemies all the (v.5) _____ all its _____ all its _____ and all the _____ of the kings of Judah.
6. You, Pashur, and all who live in your house will (v.6) _____.
7. There you will _____ and be _____.

Jeremiah's Personal Prayer

Read Jeremiah 20:7-18

Jeremiah poured his heart out to God. Notice the three verses in the middle of this passage, verses 11-13. In the midst of his pain and suffering, Jeremiah still kept his faith in God.

Jeremiah knows that (v.11-13):

- The Lord is with him like a mighty warrior
- His persecutors would not prevail, in fact they will fail and be thoroughly disgraced
- God sees and judges the hearts and minds of all people
- God will punish the wicked
- He has committed his life to God

All who are followers of Christ need to have the same confidence that Jeremiah had. Take a few minutes to go through the bullet points above. Ask yourself if you are convinced that they are true for you too. If not, ask the Lord to give you that assurance. He will.

Read Jeremiah 8:21-9:3

8. Because this passage talks about weeping, Jeremiah is often referred to as "the weeping prophet." Who is weeping in these verses, Jeremiah or God? (9:3b) _____

In 1 Samuel, we read about David the shepherd boy who later became king. He knew what it was like to have enemies. At one point, David was forced to hide out in the desert while the king (King Saul) was trying to kill him. (1 Samuel 23:14-15) But David was a praying man. He knew that His God was with him. David had spent some quality time with God out under the stars while he was watching the sheep.

We can learn a lesson from both David and Jeremiah. Spending time with God in prayer and bible study will build up our faith. Then, no matter what circumstances we face, we will have peace knowing that God is on our side. Nothing is too difficult for Him.

> *"Why are you so downcast, O my soul? Why so disturbed within me?*
> *Put your hope in God, for I will yet praise Him, my Savior and my God."*
> *Psalm 43:5*

Week Three: Day Three – Seventy Years of Captivity

Read Jeremiah 25:1-14

Jeremiah was now in his 23rd year of prophetic ministry. He was in his forties. We know that Jeremiah will prophesy over 40 years, so we have moved quickly into the second half of his prophetic ministry. It's interesting to note that just as in the four gospels of Jesus, the events at the end of Jeremiah's ministry are given the most attention in the book of Jeremiah.

Today we are reading about events that happened in the 4th year of Jehoiakim, and the first year of Nebuchadnezzar. Daniel 1:1 says that Nebuchadnezzar came to Jerusalem and besieged it in the 3rd year of Jehoiakim's reign. The siege most likely occurred at the very end of Jehoiakim's 3rd year, and the beginning of the 4th year. These prophetic words of Jeremiah in Chapter 25 must have happened literally days before the events they described took place.

1. Who does God call his servant? (v.9) _____
2. How many years will the nation of Judah serve the king of Babylon? (v.11) _____
3. What will happen at the end of the 70 years? (v.12) _____
   _____

God had given the Israelites a pre-determined number of years that they would remain in captivity. This prophecy was given before anyone had actually been captured or deported. In the days ahead, God's people who were living in Babylon during the captivity, would cling to these words of Jeremiah. The "70 years of captivity" prophecy is recorded by Daniel, Ezra, and 2 Chronicles.

<u>A peak ahead to see the fulfillment of the 70 years prophecy!</u>

We know from recorded world history, that the Babylonian empire came to an end after 70 years, when the Persians and Medes formed a partnership and conquered the Babylonians. Darius, (a Mede) was made ruler, as well as Cyrus (a Persian). (Encyclopedia Britannica; The History of Ancient Mesopotamia to the end of the Neo-Assyrian Empire 746-609)

The Prophet Daniel

One Israelite who was deported to Babylon in the 1ˢᵗ deportation, was a teenage boy named Daniel. Daniel was selected to be brought to Nebuchadnezzar's palace, because he fit the requirements – young man without physical defect, handsome, showing aptitude for learning, well-informed, quick to understand, and qualified to serve in the king's palace. Daniel lived in Babylon, but resolved to remain true to His God, and not to defile himself with the Babylonian food and wine. (See Daniel 1:1-8)

Daniel would live through the entire Babylonian captivity of the Israelites. When he was an old man, he still remembered the prophecy of Jeremiah, and witnessed the Babylonian empire being handed over to others.

Read Daniel 9:1-19

4. What did Daniel understand from the Scriptures? (v.2) _____
    _____

Notice what Daniel did when he realized that 70 years had gone by since his people had been deported. (v.3)

5. "So I _____ to the Lord God
    and _____ with him
    in _____ and _____
    and in _____ and _____."

We can learn a great deal from Daniel's prayer. Let's look at Daniel's prayer again and carefully consider what he included in it.

*   He began by praising God, and acknowledging that God had kept his word.

55

- He confessed and repented of specific sins on behalf of his people. Notice the word "we" not "I".
- He reminded God that He is always righteous, and full of mercy and forgiveness.
- He knew that the punishment that they had suffered was a direct result of their disobedience.
- He asked God to turn away his anger, not because they deserved it, but because of His righteousness.
- He asked God to open his eyes to see the desolation of the city that bears His Name.
- He reminded God again that it is not because they were righteous, but because of God's great mercy that He should help them.

Daniel ended his prayer with this final thought. He said (paraphrasing) "God, even if you don't want to do this for us, do it for your name's sake. Remember your great name. We are your people – called by your name."

Jesus also spoke about the importance of His name. He told us to use His name when we pray. There is power in the name of Jesus.

> *"And I will do whatever you ask in my name, so that the Son may bring glory to the Father" John 14:13*

> *"By faith in the name of Jesus, this man whom you see and know was made strong. It is Jesus' name and the faith that comes through him that has given this complete healing to him, as you can all see." Acts 3:16*

> *"Therefore God exalted him to the highest place and gave him the name that is above every name, that at the name of Jesus every knee should bow, in heaven and on earth and under the earth, and every tongue confess that Jesus Christ is Lord, to the glory of God the Father." Philippians 2:9-11*

When we pray in the name of Jesus, we are remembering that we are guaranteed certain privileges because we are in covenant with God the Father through Jesus. Jesus has given us His name as a guarantee. We are essentially saying the same thing as Daniel, "God, even if you don't want to do this for me, do it because of Jesus, and for His name's sake."

Now let's return to Babylon. Cyrus (a Persian), and Darius (a Mede) were each given a part of the empire to rule. This happened in 539 BC. A year later in 538 BC Cyrus gave a decree that the Jewish people could return to Jerusalem and rebuild the Temple.

Read Ezra 1:1-4

Two years before his death in 536 BC, Daniel would be alive to hear this proclamation by Cyrus and to see the people go back with Ezra to begin to rebuild. Daniel saw God fulfill the promise made through Jeremiah that there would be "seventy years in captivity".

Daniel also knew that God had heard and answered his personal prayer.

6.   When you pray, do you expect God to answer? Can you think of a specific prayer that God answered for you personally?

_____

_____

We need to pray with faith, believing that we will receive an answer from God.

> *"Therefore I tell you, whatever you ask for in prayer, believe that you have received it and it will be yours." Mark 11:24*

> *"But when he asks, he must believe and not doubt, because he who doubts is like a wave of the sea, blown and tossed by the wind. That man should not think he will receive anything from the Lord; he is a double-minded man, unstable in all he does." James 1:6-7*

Read Jeremiah 36:1-32

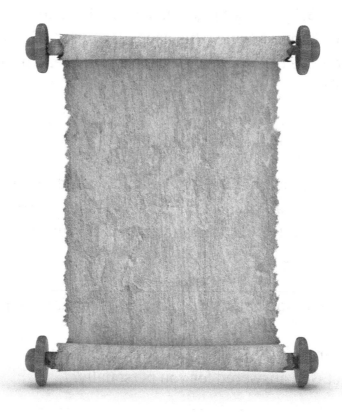

This chapter begins again during the 4ᵗʰ year of Jehoiakim. But these events happen AFTER the city of Jerusalem has been besieged and the first deportation of Daniel and others had taken place. King Jehoiakim believed that Nebuchadnezzar had already taken everything in that first deportation that he would want from Jerusalem, and therefore wouldn't be coming back. He surrounded himself with false prophets and leaders who told him whatever he wanted to hear.

Jeremiah began to dictate his messages to a scribe named Baruch, who wrote them down on a scroll. Baruch then took the scroll to the Temple courts where he read aloud the words on the scroll to the people. This must have occurred over many months, because we see in verse 9, that the date leaped ahead to the 5ᵗʰ year of Jehoiakim, in the 9ᵗʰ month. Baruch would probably read one message at a time, and so over the course of a year, if people came regularly to the Temple, they would have heard all of Jeremiah's messages at least once.

1. What reason did Jeremiah give for not going and reading the scroll himself? (v.5)

   _____

   _____

2. Where did Baruch go to read the words on the scroll? (v.10)

   _____

   _____

3. What was the response of the officials when Baruch came to them and read the scroll? (v. 16)

   _____

   _____

4. How did the king or his attendants react when they heard all of these words? (v.24)

   _____

   _____

5. What was Jerahmeel commanded to do by the king? (v.26)

   _____

   _____

6. What did Jeremiah and Baruch do after the burning of the scroll? (v.32)

   _____

   _____

King Jehoiakim thought that by burning the scroll, he would put a stop to Jeremiah's message. How different Jehoiakim was from his father! When King Josiah heard the words that had been on a different scroll, he tore his clothes and began a huge nationwide revival. His son did not learn from his example. Jehoiakim actually thought he could destroy the Word of God.

Similarly in Jesus' day, the rulers and teachers of the law after the Resurrection tried to stop the Word of God from being spoken. When Peter and the disciples began preaching that Jesus had risen from the dead, they were arrested and later released.

> *"'But to stop this thing from spreading any further among the people, we must warn these men to speak no longer to anyone in this name.' Then they called them in again and commanded them not to speak or teach at all in the name of Jesus." Acts 4:16-18*

Read Jeremiah 45:1-5

Baruch began to feel sorry for himself. He says he is "worn out with groaning". Jeremiah responded with a special word from the Lord especially for Baruch. It's noteworthy that God doesn't comfort Baruch with soothing words. Rather, God tells him that the prophecies he had written down on the scroll were true, and everything would happen just as He had said. God also told Baruch that he would have God's protection.

In much the same way, Jesus spoke to his disciples the night He was betrayed, and he didn't give them soothing words either. He told them the truth.

> *"If the world hates you, keep in mind that it hated me first. If you belonged to the world, it would love you as its own. As it is, you do not belong to the world, but I have chosen you out of the world. That is why the world hates you." John 15:18*

> *"They will treat you this way because of my name, for they do not know the One who sent me." John 15:21*

> *"They will put you out of the synagogue; in fact, a time is coming when anyone who kills you will think he is offering a service to God." John 16:2-3*

But Jesus left us with this comforting promise:

> *"I have told you these things so that in me you may have peace. In this*
> *world you will have trouble. But take heart! I have overcome the world."*
> *John 16:33*

Christians, take heart, our Lord is coming back soon! This time He'll come not to suffer, but to reign as the Mighty King of Heaven and Earth. What a great day we have in store for all of us who have placed our faith in the Lord Jesus Christ. Be comforted with these words.

> *"Every knee will bow in heaven and on earth and under the earth, and*
> *every tongue will confess that Jesus Christ is Lord, to the glory of God the*
> *Father." Philippians 2:10-11*

> *"Do not let your hearts be troubled. Trust in God; trust also in me. In my*
> *Father's house are many rooms; if it were not so, I would have told you. I*
> *am going there to prepare a place for you. And if I go and prepare a place*
> *for you, I will come back and take you to be with me that you also may be*
> *where I am." John 14:1-3*

Week Three: Day Five – Two Baskets of Figs

Read 2 Kings 24:1-6, 8-17

So far in our reading we have seen two deportations:

- The 1ˢᵗ deportation was in 605 BC (*Daniel and others, and some valuable articles*) during King Jehoiakim's reign. This was a small deportation compared to the others.
- The 2ⁿᵈ deportation was in 597 BC after Jehoiakim's death, when his son, King Jehoiachin, surrendered to Nebuchadnezzar. (*Ezekiel the prophet, 10,000 captives, an army of 7000, some articles from the temple*) This was the largest deportation of people.

By the year 597 BC (the year of the 2ⁿᵈ deportation), Jeremiah had been prophesying for approximately 30 years. He was watching as the events he had been prophesying were literally happening in front of his eyes.

With King Jehoiakim and his son King Jehoiachin gone within a few months of each other, Jehoiakim's brother Zedekiah became the new king. He was the third son of Josiah to be king – and the last.

Read Jeremiah 24:1-10

Jeremiah was walking by the entrance to the Temple and saw two baskets of figs. One basket had very good figs, and the other was so bad they couldn't be eaten.

1. Who did the good figs represent? (v. 5)

    _____

    _____

2. What will God do for the good figs? (v. 6-7)

    _____

    _____

3. Who do the poor figs represent? (v. 8)

    _____

    _____

4. How will God deal with the poor figs? (v. 9-10)

    _____

    _____

Jesus also used parables to illustrate a lesson. In one occasion He described a future time when He will return to sit on His throne in glory. He said that He will separate all people into two groups – sheep and goats. Just like the good figs and the poor figs, God will treat each of these two groups differently.

Read Matthew 25:31-46

The sheep (those who have fed the hungry, sheltered strangers, clothed the poor, looked after the sick, and visited prisoners) will be blessed. They will take their inheritance - the kingdom prepared for them since the creation of the world.

The goats (those who didn't feed the hungry, shelter strangers, clothe the poor, look after the sick or visit prisoners) will be cursed. They will go into the eternal fire prepared for the devil and his angels.

5. Based on what we know about God's faithfulness to keep His Word, how likely is it that we will see people separated into two groups like sheep and goats one day in the future?

_____

_____

We know that we are not saved by our works. Doing good deeds is not going to get us into heaven. But good deeds are evidence of our faith. They prove that we are followers of Christ.

"Suppose a brother or sister is without clothes and daily food. If one of you says to him, "Go, I wish you well; keep warm and well fed," but does nothing about his physical needs, what good is it? In the same way, faith by itself, if it is not accompanied by action, is dead. But someone will say, "You have faith; I have deeds." Show me your faith without deeds, and I

will show you my faith by what I do. You believe that there is one God.
Good! Even the demons believe that - and shudder....As the body without
the spirit is dead, so faith without deeds is dead." James 2:15-19, 26

6. Have you done anything recently that would include you in the "sheep"
    group? For instance, have you fed the hungry, clothed the naked, visited
    the prisoners, etc.? Name some of your good deeds here.

    _____

    _____

Those of us who want to be included in the "sheep" group can begin today to
ask God what He would have us do to show His kindness and mercy. Simple acts
of kindness can display His love and mercy to the world without preaching a
single word.

7. Is there an opportunity this week for you to show God's kindness?

    _____

    _____

8. Is there an opportunity soon for you and your small group to serve
    together?

    _____

    _____

"If you spend yourselves in behalf of the hungry and satisfy the needs of
the oppressed, then your light will rise in the darkness, and your night will
become like the noonday." Isaiah 58:10

"Command them to do good, to be rich in good deeds and to be generous
and willing to share." 1 Timothy 6:18

WEEK THREE- SMALL GROUP DISCUSSION –
A Message of Life and Death

Open in Prayer.

Review Questions:

1. Discuss what you have learned so far about Jeremiah:
    *   His personal relationship with God
    *   His personal life
    *   His relationships with people

2. What do you remember about these messages or illustrations?
    *   The message of impending disaster
    *   70 years of captivity
    *   The baskets of figs

3. Discuss the persecution of Jeremiah
    *   Why did Pashur the priest put Jeremiah in stocks?
    *   Why did the people want to sentence him to death?
    *   Why was the scroll burned? By who?

4. How does the church face persecution today?
5. Discuss what you have learned about the 1st and 2nd deportations.
    *   When did they happen?
    *   Who was deported?
    *   What events led to each deportation?

6. Have you found Jesus yet in the book of Jeremiah? (We will look at this in more detail in Week Seven)

Like Jeremiah, Christians bring a message of both life and death.

7. Read Romans 2:5-11. What is the message we bring to those who **reject** the Truth of the Gospel?

8. Read Romans 3:21-24. What is the message we bring to those who have received Jesus Christ by faith?
9. Read Matthew 25:1-13. Jesus tells the parable of the Ten Virgins. This is a message of both life and death. What happens to the foolish virgins? What happens to the wise virgins?

It is foolish for anyone to procrastinate and think that on a future day he will make a decision to follow Christ. No one knows the day or the hour that the Lord will come back. Once He returns it will be too late. If you haven't yet prayed the prayer of repentance and asked Jesus Christ to be the Lord of your life, do it today. It is a matter of life or death. Ask your small group to pray with you.

Read these parables of Jesus. All of them have a message of death and a message of life. After you read the parable out loud, decide what each parable teaches about death and life.

Luke 8:4-15   The Sower and his Seed
Luke 12:16-21   The Rich Man
Luke 12:35-40   The Watchful Servants
Luke 13:23-30   The Narrow Door
Luke 16:19-31   The Rich Man and Lazarus

Here are a few verses that include both a message of life and a message of death:

"See now that I myself am He! There is no God besides me. I put to death and I bring to life, I have wounded and I will heal, and no one can deliver out of my hand." Deuteronomy 32:39

"For the upright will live in the land, and the blameless will remain in it; but the wicked will be cut off from the land, and the unfaithful will be torn from it." Proverbs 2:21-22

"The truly righteous man attains life, but he who pursues evil goes to his death." Proverbs 11:19

"Tell the righteous it will be well with them for they will enjoy the fruit of their deeds. Woe to the wicked! Disaster is upon them! They will be paid back for what their hands have done." Isaiah 3:10-11

"Blessed are those who wash their robes that they may have the right to the tree of life and may go through the gates into the city. Outside are the dogs, those who practice magic arts, the sexually immoral, the murderers, the idolaters and everyone who loves and practices falsehood." Revelation 22:14-15

As you end your small group discussion for Week Three, take time to pray for one another, encouraging and strengthening each other.

WEEK FOUR

King Zedekiah's Reign

Day One – The Yoke

Some time has passed. Jeremiah is fifty years old. It is now the 4th year of King Zedekiah's reign. Zedekiah is only twenty-five years old and he has seen his people deported to Babylon twice, including his brother and his nephew.

Read Jeremiah 27:1-22

A **yoke** is "a device for joining together a pair of animals, especially oxen, usually consisting of a crosspiece with two bow-shaped pieces, each enclosing the head of an animal." (dictionary.com)

Yokes were used to control animals mostly for the purpose of plowing, to make the animal move in the direction its master wanted it to go. The wearer of a yoke is the servant to whoever has control of the yoke.

1. What is Jeremiah commanded to do? (v. 2)

_____

_____

2. List the countries whose king Jeremiah sent word to: (v.3)

*   _____

*   _____

*   _____

*   _____

*   _____

The nations of Edom, Moab and Ammon were located along the southern and eastern border of Judah. During the reign of Solomon, their lands had all been part of Israel. Tyre and Sidon were fortified cities to the north along the coastline of the Mediterranean Sea. They both belonged to the nation of Phoenicia.

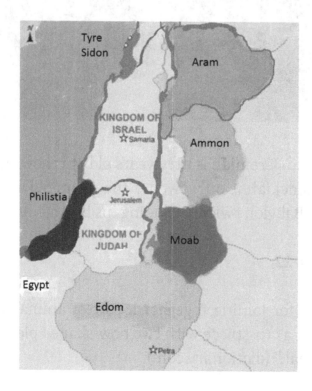

God had a message for these nations.

3.   I made the (v.5) _____ its _____
     and the _____ that are on it.
4.   I give it to _____ I please.
5.   Now I will hand all of your countries over to my servant, _____
     _____.
6.   Even the _____
     will be subject to him.
7.   If any nation refuses to serve Nebuchadnezzar or bow its neck under
     his yoke (v.8), _____
     _____.
8.   Do not listen to (v.9) _____.
9.   If your nation will bow its neck under the yoke of the king of
     Babylon and serve him, God will let that nation (v.11)_____
     _____
10. Besides these nations, who else received this same message? (v. 12)
     _____
11. What would happen to the rest of the articles of furnishings from
     Solomon's Temple and the palace of the king? (v.22)_____
     _____

Jesus also used the illustration of a yoke in His teaching. He said that His yoke was easy.

> "Come to me, all you who are weary and burdened, and I will give you rest. Take my **yoke** upon you and learn from me, for I am gentle and humble in heart, and you will find rest for your souls. For my **yoke** is easy and my burden is light." Matthew 11:28-30

Jesus said that when we take His yoke, and give up trying to go our own way; when we learn to trust that He knows better than we do which path we should take - then we will find that His way is the way of peace and rest. To be yoked together with Jesus, is to enter the "rest of God".

"There remains, then, a Sabbath-rest for the people of God; for anyone who enters God's rest also rests from his own work, just as God did from his. Let us, therefore, make every effort to enter that rest, so that no one will fall by following their example of disobedience." Hebrews 4:9-11

Obedience is the key to being yoked with Jesus. Obedience was also the key for King Zedekiah and the surrounding nations. Unfortunately, they refused to take the yoke.

Jesus offers His yoke to anyone who wants to enter God's rest. All it requires is obedience! It means following God wherever He goes, rather than going in our own direction. We need to stop resisting the pull of the yoke and let Him lead. If we want to enter His rest, we need to take His yoke. It's that simple.

I believe all true followers of Christ want to obey God. Our intentions are good. We would like to take the yoke that Jesus spoke of and learn of Him. But when temptations come along, because our human nature (or carnal nature) is still alive and well, we sometimes find ourselves giving in to the temptation resulting in sin. How can we learn to stop indulging our sin nature? How can we make our sin nature come under submission to our spiritual nature?

The Holy Spirit will be our Teacher and our Guide. He will teach us to live by the spirit, and not by the flesh. If we want to conform to the image of Jesus we cannot possibly hope to achieve that goal apart from the Holy Spirit. He has the power to overcome any temptation and He will help us if we seek Him with our whole heart. We need to be willing. Sometimes we need to humble ourselves and ask God for help.

"So I say, live by the Spirit, and you will not gratify the desires of the sinful nature. For the sinful nature desires what is contrary to the Spirit, and the Spirit what is contrary to the sinful nature. They are in conflict with each other, so that you do not do what you want." Galatians 5:16-17

"Do not conform any longer to the pattern of this world, but be transformed by the renewing of your mind. Then you will be able to test and approve what God's will is - his good, pleasing and perfect will." Romans 12:2

Read Jeremiah 28:1-17

Today's reading in Chapter 28 follows immediately after the events in Chapter 27. Notice that it is still the 4th year of Zedekiah's reign. We are introduced to a new character, Hananiah, a prophet from Gibeon. His name means, "Yahweh is gracious".

In all appearances, Hananiah seemed to be a true prophet. He began his message with "This is what the Lord Almighty, the God of Israel, says." He took the illustration that Jeremiah had used of a "yoke" and gave his own interpretation of how a yoke would be used. He said that God would break the yoke of the king of Babylon – just the opposite of Jeremiah's message. Two months later, Hananiah died. (v. 17)

1. What was Hananiah's message?
   - I will break the yoke of the king of Babylon within_____ years.
   - I will bring back _____
   - I will also bring back _____ and _____.

As if it wasn't difficult enough to prophecy about God's impending judgment, Jeremiah also had the added challenge of false prophets like Hananiah who gave the people a false message! Jeremiah told the people to surrender to Nebuchadnezzar. Hananiah told them to resist and not to surrender. Whose voice should the people listen to? It must have been very confusing for the people of that day.

Read Jeremiah 14:13-16

Jeremiah had to stand firm, knowing that he was right and the false prophets were not. He was speaking the truth. Someday the people would realize that the other prophets were lying.

Read Jeremiah 6:13-16

Jeremiah is a wonderful role-model for those of us who live in the current post-Christian world. We too must learn to stand firm, knowing that we have the Truth on our side. Jesus is the Way, the Truth, and the Life. No man comes to the Father but through Him – period. (See John 14:6)

> *"Preach the Word; be prepared in season and out of season; correct, rebuke and encourage-with great patience and careful instruction. For the time will come when men will not put up with sound doctrine. Instead, to suit their own desires, they will gather around them a great number of teachers to say what their itching ears want to hear. They will turn their ears away from the truth and turn aside to myths." 2 Timothy 4:2-4*

We must follow Jeremiah's example. Followers of Christ will "correct, rebuke, encourage with great patience and careful instruction." Have courage! We have the Truth with us. His name is Jesus.

2. Are there people in your life that oppose the Word of God?

   _____

   _____

Week Four: Day Three – City Under Siege Again!

Read Jeremiah 21:1-14

Remember Pashur? (See Week Three Day Two) He was the priest that had Jeremiah beaten and put in stocks during the reign of Jehoiakim. Now Pashur went to visit Jeremiah at the command of King Zedekiah, along with another priest, Zephaniah. Isn't this a remarkable turn of events? As far as we can tell from Scripture, the king never acknowledged that Jeremiah had been mistreated, or that some of the prophecies of Jeremiah had proven to be true. Jeremiah should have been honored and respected as a prophet of God. Instead he and his message were rejected by the king and the priests.

But suddenly, King Zedekiah wanted Jeremiah to inquire of the Lord for him. He realized that they were in big trouble, and events were happening exactly as Jeremiah had prophesied. The Babylonian army was back, and had laid siege again around Jerusalem. But why ask Jeremiah? Shouldn't Pashur and Zephaniah (both priests) be inquiring of the Lord themselves? We know from Jeremiah 20:6 that Pashur had been prophesying lies. That might make it difficult for him to inquire of the Lord!

If the King had wanted to inquire of the Lord, all he would have to do was read the scroll that Jeremiah and Baruch had written. Oh wait! Uncle Jehoiakim had burned the scroll.

Jeremiah's message had been clear and consistent for more than 30 years. The fact that Nebuchadnezzar was at the city gates again, seemed to get Zedekiah's attention. Where did he turn for advice when there was no one else who could help? Jeremiah, of course.

1. What were they hoping God would do? (v.2)
   _____
   _____

2. Who was going to fight against them? (v.5)
   _____
   _____

3. Those who choose to stay in the city will (v.9)
   _____
   _____

4. Whoever (v.9) _____
   will live, he will escape with his life.

Why is it that people turn to God in prayer only when they have exhausted every other possibility?

5. Have you ever called out to God in desperation only after trying everything else first?
   _____
   _____

It is important that God's people pray at all times – not just as a last resort! The Holy Spirit will lead us when we look first to Him.

Read Jeremiah 34:1-7

6. What did Jeremiah say to King Zedekiah:
    - Regarding Jerusalem (v.2) _____
    - Regarding his capture (v.3) _____
    - Regarding his own death _____

"And pray in the Spirit on all occasions with all kinds of prayers and requests." Ephesians 6:18a

Read Jeremiah 37:1-21

Jerusalem was still under siege by the Babylonian army. Jeremiah was free to come and go among the people. Then all of a sudden one day, Pharaoh led his army out of Egypt and King Nebuchadnezzar panicked. He withdrew his army from Jerusalem in a hurry because he thought the Egyptian army was coming to rescue King Zedekiah and the people of Judah.

Meanwhile, Jeremiah learned that a share of some property in his hometown of Anathoth, belonged to him. He decided to go there and find out more about the property. As he was walking out of the city, past the city gate, he was arrested.

1. What reason did they give for arresting him? (v. 13)

   _____

   _____

The officials were so angry at Jeremiah that they had him beaten, and put in a vaulted cell in a dungeon where he remained for "a long time". Meanwhile,

King Zedekiah decided that he wanted a secret conversation with Jeremiah in person. He sent for Jeremiah so that he could speak to him privately.

2. What did the king ask Jeremiah in their private meeting? (v.17)

    _____

    _____

Verse 20 gives us some insight into how bad the living conditions were in the dungeon.

3. Jeremiah said, "Do not send me back to the house of Jonathan the secretary or _____

    _____

4. As a result of his petition, what did the king do for Jeremiah? (v.21)

    _____

    _____

5. Use your imagination to describe the living conditions in the dungeon.

    _____

    _____

6. Can you relate to Jeremiah? Think of a time when you faced a situation that you thought you wouldn't survive.

    _____

    _____

The apostle Paul and others have endured life threatening experiences because of their faith in Jesus.

> *"We were under great pressure, far beyond our ability to endure, so that we despaired even of life. Indeed, in our hearts we felt the sentence of death. But this happened that we might not rely on ourselves but on God, who raises the dead. He has delivered us from such a deadly peril, and he will deliver us. On him we have set our hope*

that He will continue to deliver us as you help us by your prayers."
2 Corinthians 1:8b-11a

Do you ever get discouraged? Sometimes the challenges of life can get us down. Thankfully, the Bible shares with us some personal stories of men and women, and the difficult challenges they faced to encourage us. Take Joseph and Ruth for example.

Joseph, son of Jacob

His own brothers were so jealous that they wanted to kill him, but decided to sell him to the Ishmaelites who took him to Egypt.

> *"Here comes that dreamer!' they said to each other. 'Come now, let's kill him and throw him into one of these cisterns and say that a ferocious animal devoured him. Then we'll see what comes of his dreams."*
> *Genesis 37:19*

Instead of turning his back on God and complaining about his situation, Joseph chose to trust in God. He did his best to obey God. When Potiphar's wife made advances toward him, Joseph said,

> *"My master has withheld nothing from me except you, because you are his wife. How then could I do such a wicked thing and sin against God?"*
> *Genesis 39:9b*

In Egypt (although he had been sold into slavery), Joseph remained faithful to God. And God remained faithful to Joseph.

> *"The Lord blessed the household of the Egyptian because of Joseph. The blessing of the Lord was on everything Potiphar had, both in the house and in the field. So he left in Joseph's care everything he had; with Joseph in charge, he did not concern himself with anything except the food he ate." Genesis 39:5-6*

God was with Joseph, and had a good plan for his life, but his circumstances weren't always easy. This is true for all of us. We can count on our God, in any situation we may face, through the good times and the bad. God knew that one day Joseph would be ruling Egypt – second only to the Pharaoh, himself. One day Joseph would understand why he was brought to Egypt. But in the meantime, he had to put his hope in God.

Ruth, a Moabite

Ruth married into a family that had come to Moab from Bethlehem because of a famine. I'm sure that on her wedding day, Ruth had planned to live happily ever after with her new husband. However, after ten years, they were struck by tragic circumstances. While still living in Moab, Ruth's husband, her brother-in-law, and her father-in-law all died. Ruth had to make a decision. She could either stay in Moab and look for a new husband, or return to Bethlehem with her mother-in-law, Naomi.

Ruth also had a choice to make about God. If she stayed in Moab she would return to the Moabite gods. But if she went with Naomi, she would continue to serve the Living God of Israel, whom she had come to know over the past ten years through her husband's family. By staying with Naomi, she made a choice about which God she would worship and obey.

> "Ruth replied, "Don't urge me to leave you or to turn back from you. Where you go I will go, and where you stay I will stay. Your people will be my people and **your God my God**." Ruth 1:16

These were difficult decisions for Ruth. Her circumstances were dire. Naomi had no source of income. Ruth would be providing not only for herself, but also for her mother-in-law. What chances would she have to find another husband? What hope would there be that she would ever have children of her own? Her situation seemed hopeless.

But God was with her. Remember, Ruth wasn't even an Israelite! She was a Moabite woman – yet she placed her faith in the God of Abraham, Isaac, and

Jacob. This is comforting to anyone who was not born a Jew! Anyone may come to the Savior Jesus Christ. He died for the whole world.

You can read the rest of the story in the book of Ruth. God blessed Ruth by giving her both a wonderful husband, and a son – the future grandfather of David – the king of Israel.

> *"So Boaz took Ruth and she became his wife. Then he went to her, and the Lord enabled her to conceive, and she gave birth to a son. The women said to Naomi: 'Praise be to the Lord, who this day has not left you without a kinsman-redeemer. May he become famous throughout Israel!'" Ruth 4:13-14*

7. What is your story? What dire circumstances are you facing today?

   _____

   _____

   _____

8. When people read about your story in the years to come, will they be strengthened and encouraged in their faith by the choices you made - like Joseph, Ruth, or Jeremiah?

   _____

   _____

   _____

> *"But now, this is what the Lord says – he who created you, O Jacob, he who formed you, O Israel: Fear not, for I have redeemed you; I have summoned you by name; you are mine. When you pass through the waters, I will be with you; and when you pass through the rivers, they will not sweep over you. When you walk through the fire, you will not be burned; the flames will not set you ablaze. For I am the Lord, your God, the Holy One of Israel, your Savior...Do not be afraid, for I am with you." Isaiah 43:1-3a, 5a*

Read Jeremiah Chapter 38:1-13

Jeremiah was living in the courtyard of the guard, and most likely was speaking to anyone who passed by. Verse one says he was "telling all the people". The message Jeremiah was telling them was that they must surrender to the Babylonians if they wanted to live. He also told them that Jerusalem would be handed over to Babylon.

Pashur, his son Gedaliah, and two other priests heard what Jeremiah was saying and became very angry. They went to the king and argued that Jeremiah should be killed. They said Jeremiah was discouraging the soldiers and the people. The king gave in to their demands and said, "Do whatever you want with him."

So, they lowered Jeremiah by ropes into a cistern. The well had no water - just mud - so Jeremiah sank down deep into the mud. What a humiliating experience! Their intention was to leave him there to starve to death. But God sent a stranger to rescue Jeremiah. God will make a way when there is no way!

1. Who did God use to rescue Jeremiah? (v.7)

   _____

   _____

A "eunuch" was a term for a castrated man. Castration was a common practice in some ancient cultures. Boys that were being prepared for positions in the royal service were required to become eunuchs. Ethiopia was one of the countries that required boys to become eunuchs to keep them faithfully in the service of the king.

A side note: There was another Ethiopian eunuch mentioned in Acts 8:26 who was led to faith in Christ by Philip the apostle.

Ebed-Melech showed his kindness to Jeremiah, risking his own life by taking up the cause of our unpopular prophet. To find out what became of Ebed-Melech, read Jeremiah 39:15-18.

Read Jeremiah 38:14-28

The situation in Jerusalem had deteriorated. Zedekiah had to reconsider his difficult options. Finally, he sent for Jeremiah.

2. Had Jeremiah been consistent with his message to the king? (v.17-18)

   _____

   _____

3. What was the secret oath that King Zedekiah swore to Jeremiah? (v. 16)

   _____

   _____

4. Jeremiah told Zedekiah that (v.17-18)
   - His life would be spared if _____
   - The city would not be burned down if _____
   - The city will be handed over to the Babylonians if _____
   - The king himself will not escape if_____

5. Who was the king afraid of (v.19) and why?

   _____

   _____

6. What did Zedekiah think would happen to Jeremiah if anyone heard about their conversation? (v. 24)

   _____

   _____

Jeremiah showed great courage when he spoke with the king. King Zedekiah, on the other hand, was a coward. The king was afraid of his own people. He was clearly more afraid of men than God.

God tells us that we should not fear what man can do to us, but rather we should fear what will happen to us for all eternity.

> *"Do not be afraid of those who kill the body but cannot kill the soul. Rather, be afraid of the One who can destroy both soul and body in hell."* Matthew 10:28

7. Are you afraid of what people might say about you, or might be thinking about you? If so, when?

   _____

   _____

8. Can you think of a time in your life that you showed great courage like Jeremiah?

   _____

   _____

9. Have you ever been a coward like King Zedekiah?

   _____

   _____

10. What can you apply to your own life from the examples of these two men?

_____

_____

"Whoever acknowledges me before men, I will also acknowledge him before my Father in heaven. But whoever disowns me before men, I will disown him before my Father in heaven." Matthew 10:32-33

WEEK FOUR SMALL GROUP DISCUSSION –
COVENANT PROMISES

Open in prayer.

By the end of Week Four, we find Jerusalem and the entire kingdom of Judah, in its final hours. What led to this disaster? Let's consider how the people had broken their covenant with God. Then let's look at the terms of the New Covenant and what it means to the church today.

The Old Covenant

Read Deuteronomy 29:22-29, and 30:15-20
Read Jeremiah 11:2-8

1. What were the terms of the covenant that the people had broken?
2. What would the consequences be of their not keeping the covenant?
3. Did the people agree to this covenant?

The New Covenant

Read 1 Corinthians 11:23-26
Read Galatians 3:6-14

4. What is the New Covenant based on?
5. What is the one thing that is needed for us to receive the blessings of Abraham?

Read 1 John 1:8-10, 2:3-6

6. What do we need to do, in order to be forgiven by God?
7. What is the expectation of those who claim to know Christ?

Read 1 John 2:9-10

8. What is one clear indication that a person has come into the light?

Read Romans 10:9-11

9. How does someone enter this covenant?

Read Galatians 5:1-6

10. With this New Covenant, what is the only thing that counts (v.6)?

Read Revelation 22:1-21

11. What is the future hope for those who are partakers of the New Covenant?
    * Describe the river of the water of life and the tree of life.
    * Where will the Lamb's servants be? Where will His name be?
    * Why won't there be any need for the sun?
    * Jesus plans to give out rewards (v.12). How will He determine what rewards He will give?
    * What are we to do if we want to have the right to the tree of life and the city?
    * Who will not be allowed inside the gates?
    * Who gives us this testimony (instructions) for the church?

12. What is the warning that is given (v.18-19)?

A Review of the Old and New Covenants

13. What are the differences between the Old and New Covenants?
14. Why was there a need for a New Covenant?
15. It's unfortunately true that many Christians are still trying to live by the Old Covenant Law. Do you think the people in your church are living under the terms of the Old or New Covenant?

*"He who testifies to these things says, "Yes, I am coming soon." Amen.
Come, Lord Jesus. The grace of the Lord Jesus be with God's people. Amen."*
Revelation 22:20-21

As you end your small group discussion for Week Four, take time to pray for one another, encouraging and strengthening each other.

WEEK FIVE

A Message of Hope

DAY ONE – A PROMISE OF RESTORATION

Read Jeremiah 30:1-24

The theme this week is "Hope". We will look at several "messages of hope" Jeremiah gave that stand out as shining stars in the midst of the darkness.

Jeremiah wrote in a book, "*The days are coming when I will bring my people Israel and Judah back from captivity and restore them to the land I gave their forefathers to possess*". (v.3) God had given the land to Abraham's descendants as part of the Abrahamic Covenant.

> "*The Lord appeared to Abram and said, 'To your offspring I will give this land.'" Genesis 12:7*

<u>The Near-Far Principle of Interpretation</u>

One of the keys to understanding Biblical prophecy is to learn that God often has more than one purpose or meaning in mind. Theologians who interpret scripture refer to this double meaning in many ways. Names such as the Near-Far View, the Double Fulfillment of Prophecy, and the Double Sense Gap, are given to explain that God intended more than one meaning to His words.

The message that God gives to his prophet is intended to be interpreted by the people at the time the prophecy is given (those <u>near</u> to the prophecy) in a very literal sense, but may also have a fulfillment by future generations (those <u>far</u> from the prophecy).

Verse 7 is an example of the "Near-Far" principle.

> *"How awful that day will be! None will be like it. It will be a time of trouble for Jacob, but he will be saved out of it." Jeremiah 30:7*

Surely the day was coming to the Land of Judah that was going to be a dreadful day. The Babylonians would in fact, capture Jerusalem and burn it down. This would literally happen. But we also know that there is a future fulfillment of this verse. An awful day is coming to the whole earth in the future. Jesus spoke of that day:

> *"For then there will be great distress, unequaled from the beginning of the world until now – never to be equaled again. If those days had not been cut short, no one would survive, but for the sake of the elect those days will be shortened....Immediately after the distress of those days 'the sun will be darkened, and the moon will not give its light; the stars will fall from the sky, and the heavenly bodies will be shaken.' At that time the sign of the Son of Man will appear in the sky, and all the nations of the earth will mourn. They will see the Son of Man coming on the clouds of the sky with power and great glory." Matthew 24:21-22, 29-30*

So Jeremiah 30:7 will be fulfilled twice – once near (in 586 BC) and once more when the great tribulation that Jesus spoke of takes place on the earth.

Let's return now to Jeremiah Chapter 30. King David had been dead for 400 years at the time of this prophecy.

1. Who is Jeremiah speaking about in verses 9 and 21?

   _____

   _____

2. Instead of being enslaved by foreigners, who will the people serve? (v.9)

    _____

    _____

3. Jacob (Israel) will again have (v.10)_____

    and _____.

4. All who devour you will be (v.16) _____

5. I will restore you to (v.17) _____ and

    _____ your wounds.

6. In verse 18, God promises that the city of Jerusalem will be rebuilt on her ruins and the palace will stand in its proper place. Was that prophecy fulfilled in the past? _____

    (Matthew 24:1-2)

The temple was rebuilt in 516 BC and was completely restored by Herod the Great in 20 BC. This temple came to be known as Herod's Temple according to Josephus. Read more about the restoration of the temple in the Book of Ezra.

Read Revelation 21:2-5

7. How will this prophecy about the temple be fulfilled in the future as well? (near/far principal)

    _____

    _____

We can read this prophecy in Jeremiah and see that it can be fulfilled twice. Near - as when Ezra and Nehemiah returned to rebuild the temple and the walls of the city. Far - as it will someday be fulfilled by God when He replaces old Jerusalem with his new heavenly city. God's throne will be in Jerusalem. There will be no temple – no need for the ark, or the sacrifices, because Jesus Himself will be seated on the throne.

This prophecy gives God's people great hope. God's prophets spoke of the future dwelling of God to fill us with hope until that day comes.

"Now faith is being sure of what we hope for and certain of what we do not see. This is what the ancients were commended for." Hebrews 11:1-2

8. How does Jeremiah's message of restoration offer us hope today?

_____

_____

God had promised King David that he would always have a son to sit on the throne.

"I will raise up your offspring to succeed you who will come from your own body, and I will establish his kingdom. He is the one who will build a house for my name, and I will establish the throne of his kingdom forever. I will be his father, and he will be my son." 2 Samuel 7:12b-14a

This promise to David also has both a near/far fulfillment. His son, Solomon, sat on the throne and built the first temple. His future descendant, Jesus Christ, would also sit on a heavenly throne. He would build a dwelling – not made with hands - in the new Jerusalem.

Week Five: Day Two - A Better Covenant!

Read Jeremiah 17:10

God was searching the hearts and minds of His people. He found that their hearts were deceitful above all things and beyond cure. God saw that "Judah's sin was engraved with an iron tool" and "inscribed on the tablets of their hearts". Sin was so deeply planted in their heart that it couldn't be erased.

So He decided to offer the people a brand new heart – a "circumcised heart". And since He was creating new hearts, He would go one step further, and permanently write His law on their hearts.

Read Jeremiah 31:31-37

God's people broke the old covenant (the Mosaic Covenant) by entering into idolatry, among other things. In Chapter 31, Jeremiah reveals God's plan to make a new covenant in the future. He said, "The time is coming" when He will make a new covenant. Until that day, the people would wait with hope until the prophecy was fulfilled. Jeremiah said that someday, God would create in them a new heart, one that obeyed the law of love. He would give them a heart that would be filled with God's holiness and truth. He would give them a heart that was forgiven of all of its sins, and therefore, would forgive other people of their sins.

From our reading we can learn several things about the New Covenant.

1. The covenant will be with the both the house of (v.31) _____ _____ and the house of _____.

2. It will not be like the covenant I made with their (v.32) _____ _____ when I took them by the hand to lead them out of Egypt.

3. I will put my law in their (v. 33) _____and write it on their _____

4. I will be their God, and they will be (v.33) _____

94

5. They will all (v.34) _____
    me, from the least of them to the greatest.
6. I will (v. 34) _____ their wickedness
    and will remember their _____ no more.

<u>Let's take a peek ahead and see the fulfillment of this prophecy!</u>

Jesus and his disciples were eating the Passover Meal the night that he was betrayed. Jesus told them that this was not just another Passover Meal. It was actually the Covenant Meal. They were eating the meal that would initiate a **New Covenant** between God and men.

> *"And he took bread, gave thanks and broke it, and gave it to them saying, "This is my body given for you; do this in remembrance of me." In the same way, after the supper he took the cup, saying, "This cup is the **new covenant** in my blood, which is poured out for you." Luke 22:19-20*

Jesus was declaring that His blood would be the seal of the New Covenant spoken of in Jeremiah 31:31.

The Book of Hebrews provides us with a wonderful commentary on this prophecy.

Read Hebrews 7:18 – 8:13

The writer of Hebrews explained that Jesus is our high priest. He was not a priest according to the Levitical priesthood (under the terms of the Mosaic Covenant), but rather he was appointed to the priesthood by God Himself.

> *"But He became a priest with an oath when God said to him: "The Lord has sworn and will not change his mind: You are a priest forever." Hebrews 7:21*

<u>A Superior High Priest</u>

Hebrews describes the superiority of the priesthood that Jesus belongs to. His priesthood is permanent, because Jesus is alive for all eternity.

> *"But because Jesus lives forever, he has a permanent priesthood. Therefore he is able to save completely those who come to God through him, because he always lives to intercede for them." Hebrews 7:24-25*

Next we learn that our high priest, who is "holy, blameless, pure, and set apart from sinners," made a sacrifice "once for all when he offered Himself". (v. 27) No need for a priest to offer sacrifices daily anymore. In the making of the New Covenant, there was only one perfect sacrifice made, then our high priest sat down. He was done. When Jesus said on the cross, "It is finished", he understood that by dying once for mankind no more sacrifice would be necessary - ever again!

> *"But the ministry Jesus has received is as superior to theirs as the covenant of which he is mediator is superior to the old one, and it is founded on better promises. For if there had been nothing wrong with that first covenant, no place would have been sought for another." Hebrews 8:6-7*

7.   Jesus is superior to other high priests because (7:24)

_____

_____

<u>A Superior Covenant</u>

Read Hebrews 9:1-10

Jesus is the mediator of a superior covenant to the Old Covenant. The New Covenant makes the Old Covenant obsolete.

> *"By calling this covenant "new," he has made the first one obsolete: and what is obsolete and aging will soon disappear." Hebrews 8:13*

In the Mosaic Law, every sacrifice that was made to atone for man's sin required that an animal's blood be poured out. It was the blood of the sacrifice that made it acceptable to God. It was also the blood of these animals that was sprinkled on the priests and in the sanctuary to cleanse them from sin.

> *"For the life of a creature is in the blood, and I have given it to you to make atonement for yourselves on the altar; it is the blood that makes atonement for one's life." Leviticus 17:11*

> *"In fact the law requires that nearly everything be cleansed with blood and without the shedding of blood there is no forgiveness." Hebrews 9:22*

Jesus willingly poured out his own holy blood, to cleanse us from sin, making us acceptable to God.

<u>Superior Blood</u>

While the blood of the animal could temporarily cleanse the people outwardly, it couldn't cleanse them inwardly. Clearly, we needed help on the inside. Thanks to our high priest, Jesus, His sacrifice cleansed us completely inside and out. He made it possible for us to serve God, because we've been made holy.

> *"The blood of goats and bulls and the ashes of a heifer sprinkled on those who are ceremonially unclean sanctify them so that they are outwardly clean. How much more, then, will the blood of Christ, who through the*

*eternal Spirit offered himself unblemished to God, cleanse our consciences from acts that lead to death, so that we may serve the living God." For this reason Christ is the mediator of a **new covenant,** that those who are called may receive the promised eternal inheritance – now that he has died as a ransom to set them free from the sins committed under the first covenant." Hebrews 9:13-15*

8. The blood of Jesus is superior because

_____

_____

"Since we have a great priest over the house of God, let us draw near to God with a sincere heart in full assurance of faith..." Hebrews 10:21-22

WEEK FIVE: DAY THREE – JEREMIAH BUYS A FIELD

Read Jeremiah 32:1-15

We have skipped ahead to the tenth year of Zedekiah's reign. Since we know that King Zedekiah reigned for eleven years, it is clear that time was short, for both Zedekiah and the kingdom of Judah.

About that time, Jeremiah received a personal message from the Lord saying that his cousin Hanamel would be visiting, to find out if Jeremiah would be interested in buying a field in their hometown of Anathoth. This seemed like a strange thing to do in the midst of the siege, with the Babylonian army ready to break down the walls of the city at any moment. But God instructed Jeremiah to purchase the land. Sometimes God leads us to say and do things that don't make any sense (to us) at the time!

Jeremiah obeyed the Lord, and bought the land for seventeen shekels of silver. He put his legal document (proving ownership) in a sealed clay jar. Then Jeremiah had a conversation with God.

Read Jeremiah 32:16-25

I'm paraphrasing here. Jeremiah said to God, "Dear Lord, everything You said would happen has happened. You have done amazing things. But I'm kind of confused here, Lord. Though you are handing the city over to the Babylonians, and there is impending disaster – you want me to buy a field? Help me out here." Can you relate to Jeremiah's question?

Read God's answer Jeremiah 32:26-44

1. God said that He was about to hand the city of Jerusalem over to the Babylonians who will burn it down. What are some of the reasons He gives for doing this? (v. 30-35)

   _____

   _____

2. God goes on to say that after the burning down of the city, he will bring them back again. He gives a list of promises to the people.
   - I will surely gather them from all the lands where I banish them.
   - I will bring them (v. 37) _____ _____ and let them live in safety.
   - They will be my people and _____ _____.
   I will give them _____ so that they will always fear me for their own good and the good of their children after them.
   - I will make an everlasting _____ _____ with them.
   - I will never stop _____ to them, and I will _____ them to fear me, so that they will never turn away from me.
   - I will (v. 41) _____ in doing them _____.
   - And will assuredly plant them in this land with all my _____ _____.

The promises that are listed here in verses 37-41, are more examples of "Near-Far" prophecy. They have been partially fulfilled, but will be completely fulfilled in Christ, who is the Mediator of the New Covenant.

Jeremiah's purchase of a field was to illustrate to the people that God had not forgotten His promise to Abraham. The people could have confidence in God's promise of restoration. Not only would people be buying fields again one day, but they would pay costly silver for this valuable land. The land that was given to Abraham and his descendants would once again belong to them, and God would restore their fortunes.

"Once more fields will be bought in this land of which you say, 'It is a desolate waste, without men or animals, for it has been handed over to the Babylonians'. Fields will be bought for silver and deeds will be signed.... because I will restore their fortunes, declares the Lord." 32:43, 44

This is a message of hope for all of us. God will restore. God will rebuild.

> *"It was not through law that Abraham and his offspring received the promise that he would be heir of the world, but through the righteousness that comes by faith....Therefore, the promise comes by faith, so that it may be by grace and may be guaranteed to all Abraham's offspring – not only to those who are of the law but also to those who are of the faith of Abraham. He is the father of us all." Romans 4:13, 16*

3. According to this passage in Romans, Abraham is our father too. Abraham is not only the father of those who were given the law (Israelites), but also those who _____

_____

_____

Our God is in the restoration business! What do you hope to see God restore or rebuild?

_____

_____

_____

The prophecies about the "promised land" will be fulfilled in the future. God made a promise to Abraham and He always keeps His promises.

> *"The trees of the field will yield their fruit and the ground will yield its crops. The people will be secure in the land...I will provide for them a land renowned for its crops, and they will no longer be victims of famine." Ezekiel 34:27, 29*

> *"He will look with compassion on all her ruins, he will make her deserts like Eden, her wastelands like the garden of the Lord." Isaiah 51:3*

Week Five: Day Four – A Righteous Branch!

Read Jeremiah 23:5-6

From the family tree of King David there will come a branch. This branch of David's family tree (descendants of Judah) will resemble the rest of the tree. But it won't act like the tree. In contrast to the sin and evil deeds that the family tree normally produced, this branch will do what is just and right. And, in addition, this branch will also be called, "the Lord our Righteousness" or "Jehovah Tsidkenu." Imagine someone telling you that one of your future grandchildren is going to be called, "The Lord our Righteousness". The people of Judah who were listening to this message must have wondered how it could possibly be fulfilled. The implication is that their relative would actually be Jehovah God – the Creator.

Read Jeremiah 33:14-26

1. God said that David will never fail to have a man to _____
   _____

According to this amazing prophecy, a day is coming when a righteous "Branch" will sprout from the bloodline of David. This person will sit on the throne of his father, David. In other words, he will be a righteous person, and he will also be a king.

We also learn that the day is coming when a righteous "Branch" will present sacrifices. This means the "Branch" will be a priest.

And he will be called, "The Lord our Righteousness".

To recap: Jeremiah said that one day someone will come that will be:

- God – "the Lord our Righteousness"
- Man – from David's family
- King – sitting on the throne of the house of Israel
- Priest – presenting sacrifices

How would it be possible to be all of those things? It was impossible for someone to be both king and priest, not to mention being both man and God. This is an incredible prophecy, and must have made Jeremiah wonder how it would ever be fulfilled. We've seen that Jesus was both God and man, but let's look further into His identity as king and priest.

<u>A King</u>

When Jesus stood before Pontius Pilate before he was crucified, Pilate asked him if he was a king. Jesus replied, *"You have said so."* (Matthew 27:11) *"Above his head they placed the written charge against him: this is Jesus, the king of the Jews."* (Matthew 27:37) God's Word tells us in the book of Revelation that Jesus is the Ruler of the kings of the earth. He is not only king, He is the King of kings.

> *"He has rescued us from the dominion of darkness and brought us into the **kingdom** of the Son He loves, in whom we have redemption, the forgiveness of sins." Colossians 1:13-14*

> *"After he had provided purification for sins, he sat down at the right hand of the Majesty in Heaven." Hebrews 1:3b*

> *"On his robe and on his thigh he has this name written: **King of kings** and Lord of Lords." Revelation 19:16*

<u>A Priest</u>

A priest's main responsibility was to intercede and offer sacrifices for the sins of the people. He was the bridge or the mediator between the people and God. In our reading from Hebrews (Week Five Day Two), we learned that Jesus is not only a priest, he is the great High Priest, appointed by God offering one perfect sacrifice of Himself for all time.

> *"Who is he that condemns? Christ Jesus who died – more than that, who was raised to life is at the right hand of God and is also **interceding for us**. Who shall separate us from the love of Christ?" Romans 8:34-35a*

*"There is one God and one **mediator** between God and men, the man Christ Jesus, who gave himself as a ransom for all men." 1 Timothy 2:5-6a*

"If anybody does sin, we have one who speaks to the Father in our defense – Jesus Christ, the Righteous One. He is the atoning sacrifice for our sins, and not only for ours but also for the sins of the whole world." 1 John 2:1b-2

Amazingly, Jesus is:

- God
- man
- king
- priest

When Jeremiah described the Righteous Branch, he could only have been speaking of one person – Jesus Christ.

2. What would have to happen in order for our covenant with God through Jesus Christ to be broken? (Jeremiah 33:20-21)

_____

_____

Week Five: Day Five – Call on Me!

Read Jeremiah 33:1-11

Jeremiah was still confined to the courtyard of the guard. King Zedekiah was nearing the end of his eleven-year reign. Jeremiah continued to speak out to anyone who would listen. God said, "**Call to me** and I will answer you and tell you great and unsearchable things you do not know."

The prophet Joel was quoted by Peter:

> "**Everyone who calls** on the name of the Lord will be saved." Acts 2:21

And Paul wrote to the people in Rome:

> "the same Lord is Lord of all and richly blesses **all who call on him**, for **everyone who calls** on the name of the Lord will be saved." Romans 10:13

In other words, all you have to do is call. The message of hope that Jeremiah is bringing to the people is that God is near. All they need to do is call on Him. We have this same message today. Just like Jeremiah spoke God's message to the people from his confinement in the courtyard, God wants us to go to those who are within hearing distance, and tell them to call on the Lord.

At the beginning of Chapter 33 God spoke about the judgment coming to Judah. Then His message took a different tone, as He began to speak of peace and joy.

1. Nevertheless, I will bring health and healing to it (Jerusalem); I will heal my people and will let them enjoy (v.6) _____
   _____ and security.

2. Then this city will bring me renown (v.9) _____,
   praise and honor before all nations on earth that hear of all the good things I do for it.

105

3. And they will be in awe and will tremble at the abundant prosperity and (v. 9) _____ I provide for it.

4. There will be heard once more the sounds of (v. 11) _____ _____ and _____ _____, the voices of bride and bridegroom, and the voices of those who bring thank offerings to the house of the Lord.

Jeremiah's message makes it clear to us that God wants His children to experience His peace and His joy. Jesus told us that He would give us the gift of the Holy Spirit, so that we too could have His peace, and His joy.

"Peace I leave with you; my peace I give you. I do not give to you as the world gives. Do not let your hearts be troubled and do not be afraid."
John 14:27

"I have told you this so that my joy may be in you and that your joy may be complete." John 15:11

"But the fruit of the Spirit is love, **joy, peace,** *patience, kindness, goodness, faithfulness, gentleness and self-control." Galatians 5:22*

All of those who belong to Christ Jesus have the Holy Spirit living in them. He is the One who will fill us with peace and joy.

Read Philippians 4:6-9

5. What will the peace of God transcend? (v.7)

_____

_____

6. What will the peace of God guard? (v.7)

_____

_____

Read Psalm 16:9-11

7. When we are in God's presence, what will we be filled with? (v. 11)

    _____

    _____

8. Knowing that God will not abandon me to the grave, makes my heart what? (v. 9)

    _____

    _____

Spending time with God in prayer, in worship, or in the study of His Word will fill us with joy. These are spiritual exercises that believers need to make a part of every day. Without spending time with God you may have fleeting happiness, but you won't experience true joy. Only the Spirit of God will fill us with true joy. Joy is a result of storing our treasures in heaven. It comes from caring more about the things of God than the things of this world. When my mind is focused on God and His kingdom, suddenly the things of this world – the circumstances I face each day – don't matter as much. I can walk each day with His peace and His joy, through any of life's challenges.

> *"For the kingdom of God is not a matter of eating and drinking but of righteousness, peace and joy in the Holy Spirit." Romans 14:17*

> *"Call to me and I will answer you and tell you great and unsearchable things you do not know." Jeremiah 33:3*

WEEK FIVE SMALL GROUP DISCUSSION –
GOD IS FAITHFUL

Open in prayer.

The Book of Jeremiah has 52 chapters. This past week we looked at just 4 chapters (30 through 33, and two verses from chapter 23). There was an unmistakable message of hope. God revealed his future plans for the land of Israel. He also spoke to Jeremiah about the Messiah that would come one day.

1. Browse through Week Five, and name as many promises for the future as you are able to find.
2. How can we apply these promises to ourselves and to the church today?
   - Day One – The Promise of a coming King
   - Day Two – The Promise of a better Covenant
   - Day Three – The Promise of Restoration
   - Day Four – The Promise of a Righteous Branch, a Righteous Vine
   - Day Five – The Promise of Peace and Joy

3. What have you learned this week about God's future plans?
4. Why can we have confidence that God will keep his Word?

Read Jeremiah 31:1-6

5. What kind of love does God have for His people?
6. Name several things that will happen again (v. 4-6)

Read Jeremiah 31:7-9

7. Who will come back to Israel?
8. What will they be doing on the way back? (v. 9)

Read Jeremiah 31:10-13

9. Who is going to hear about these great things? (v.10)

10. Describe the bounty of the Lord. (v.12-14)
11. Describe how the people will feel about returning. (v.12,13)

Read Jeremiah 31:15-20

12. Verse 15 has both near and far fulfillments. What are they? (See Matthew 2:17-18)
13. Ephraim was one of Joseph's two sons. (see Genesis 41:52) Describe Ephraim's relationship with God.

Read Jeremiah 31:21-22

14. Who is the unfaithful daughter? What is God telling her to do?

Notice the last part of verse 22. The Lord will create a new thing on earth. A woman will surround a man or encompass or enclose a man. We know that a mother's womb encompasses a child. There is nothing new or unusual about that. However, there is one man-child in particular that a woman will conceive that will be quite unique. This special child will be conceived by the Holy Spirit, but encompassed by a woman. (See Luke 1:28-35)

Let's look at a psalm that will review many of the concepts we have looked at this week.

Read Psalm 89:1-52

Read the verses that have the following words in them.

Count the number of times each of these words is used.

- Faithful or faithfulness _____
- Covenant_____
- Love _____
- Throne _____
- Forever_____

15. What can we learn about God from these verses?

We see in Psalm 89 that God is faithful to keep his covenant. He is all-loving, and has all authority. His love will endure forever. His throne will endure forever. He is everlasting.

As we think about the eternal covenant that is ours through our faith in Jesus Christ, there is a wonderful promise found in verses 30-34.

16. If we forsake the law, violate His decrees, and fail to keep His commands what will happen?

17. How does this the new covenant give you assurance and comfort?

As you end your small group discussion for Week Five, take time to pray for one another, encouraging and strengthening each other.

WEEK SIX

Jerusalem Captured

Day One – Jerusalem Falls

Read Jeremiah 52:1-30

Chapter 52 is the last chapter in Jeremiah's book, but it is not the end of the story. Remember that the book of Jeremiah is not written chronologically. Rather, it is a collection of prophecies and historical accounts that need to be arranged so that we can see the correct order in which they happened.

This chapter begins with some background on King Zedekiah. We learn that his mother is Hamutal, the daughter of Jeremiah but he is not our Jeremiah, the prophet. Notice Hamutal was from Libnah. Our prophet Jeremiah was from Anathoth.

We learn in verse three that Zedekiah rebelled against the king of Babylon, which resulted in the siege that lasted for two years. The siege caused a severe famine in the city and eventually the city wall was broken through, so Zedekiah's army along with Zedekiah fled. They didn't get far, however, making it only to the plains of Jericho. This is where Zedekiah was captured, and his army was scattered.

Zedekiah and his sons were brought to Nebuchadnezzar while he was temporarily residing in the city of Riblah. Zedekiah was forced to watch as Nebuchadnezzar killed his sons and all of his officials. After this, Zedekiah's eyes were put out, and he was put in bronze shackles, and taken off to Babylon. He remained in prison until he died.

1. Which buildings did Nebuzaradan (the commander of the Babylonian army) set fire to? (v. 13)

   _____

   _____

2. Who was left in the city? (v. 16)

   _____

   _____

Here is a list of all of the articles that were carried away to Babylon from the Temple of the Lord:

1. The bronze from the pillars and movable stands
2. The bronze from the bronze Sea
3. Pots, shovels, wick trimmers, sprinkling bowls, dishes and all the bronze articles used in the temple service.

4. Basins, censers, sprinkling bowls, pots, lampstands, dishes and bowls used for drink offerings – these were all made of pure gold or silver

5. Bronze from the two pillars, the Sea and the twelve bronze bulls under it and the movable stands that King Solomon had made (more than could be weighed)

6. 96 bronze pomegranates that were used to decorate the outside entrance to the temple above the pillars on the sides

7. 100 bronze pomegranates above the surrounding network

Try to imagine what that deportation looked like!

The entire Babylonian army, 745 Jews and all of the bronze, gold and silver from the Temple (v. 30) were a part of this 3rd deportation.

Let's go back 400 years to the building of Solomon's temple, to gain some insight into the value of these articles that were carried off by the Babylonians.

Read 1 Kings 7:13-51

It took Solomon seven years to complete the building of the temple. Solomon's temple was a spectacular building. It was built out of the sturdiest cedar from Lebanon. The inner sanctuary was completely covered with gold. Once the temple and its furniture were completed, Solomon went on to build himself a palace and kept acquiring more and more wealth.

"When the queen of Sheba saw all the wisdom of Solomon and the palace he had built, the food on his table, the seating of his officials, the attending servants in their robes, his cupbearers, and the burnt offerings he made at the temple of the Lord she was overwhelmed. She said to the king, "The report I heard in my own country about your achievements and your wisdom is true. But I did not believe these things until I came and saw with my own eyes. Indeed, not even half was told me; in wisdom and wealth you have far exceeded the report I heard". 1 Kings 10:6-7

"and she gave the king 120 talents of gold, large quantities of spices, and precious stones. Hiram's ships brought gold from Ophir; and from there they brought great cargoes of almugwood and precious stones...the weight of the gold that Solomon received yearly was 666 talents, not including the revenues from merchants and traders and from all the Arabian kings and the governors of the land." 1 Kings 10:10, 14

King Solomon was *"greater in riches and wisdom than all the other kings of the earth. The whole world sought audience with Solomon to hear the wisdom God had put in his heart".* (1 Kings 10:23-24) Along with wisdom, God had given Solomon enormous wealth.

> *"Year after year, everyone who came brought a gift - articles of silver and gold, robes, weapons and spices, and horses and mules....the king made silver as common in Jerusalem as stones, and cedar as plentiful as sycamore-fig trees in the foothills." 1 Kings 10:25,27*

That was in the year 992 BC. Fast forward 400 years to 587 BC. Solomon's temple had been the pride of Israel for 400 years. The articles of gold and silver used in the temple were symbolic of the wealth that God had given to Solomon. And now it was all being carried off to Babylon. The temple had been burned down.

Read Jeremiah 7:1-15

For many years Jeremiah had warned the people saying "Reform your ways and your actions and I will let you live in this place". The people had every opportunity to change and repent, but instead they continued to provoke God. The day finally came when the people of Judah witnessed their city – the City of David – burning to the ground. The temple set on fire. The articles in the temple were stolen and taken to Babylon. The people too, were bound in chains and taken into captivity.

3. How do you think the people felt
    - Toward Nebuchadnezzar? _____
    - Toward King Zedekiah? _____
    - Toward Jeremiah? _____
    - Toward God? _____

Read Jeremiah 40:1-6

Isn't this an amazing turn of events? The king of Judah, its army, and all of its officials were fleeing the country as fast as they could go. Jeremiah had been bound in chains along with the other people who were going to be deported to Babylon. Then something very strange happened.

The commander of the Babylonian army, Nebuzaradan, came searching for Jeremiah. And when he found him, he set Jeremiah free! This was the first freedom Jeremiah had known since the beginning of Zedekiah's reign (Jer. 37:16, 21) While everyone else was being put in chains and taken prisoner, Jeremiah received his freedom. The people who were in chains being deported were the very people that had heard Jeremiah preach while he was confined to the palace courtyard. I wonder if the people remembered how they had disregarded Jeremiah's warnings. More importantly, did they realize his prophecies had been right.

There were other people in the Bible who were in chains, then miraculously set free. God often used the breaking of chains to demonstrate His great power, and show that no chains can bind Him. We know that satan has no power over God's people.

- Joseph (Genesis 41:14, 41-2) *"So Pharaoh sent for Joseph, and he was quickly brought from the dungeon....Pharaoh said to Joseph, I hereby put you in charge of the whole land of Egypt."*
- Daniel (Daniel 6:16, 21-22) *"So the king gave the order, and they brought Daniel and threw him into the lions' den...Daniel answered, 'O king, live forever! My God sent his angel and he shut the mouths of the lions. They have not hurt me, because I was found innocent in his sight.'"*
- Peter and John (Acts 4:3-4) *"They seized Peter and John, and because it was evening, they put them in jail until the next day. But many who heard the message believed, and the number of men grew to about five thousand."*
- The Apostles (Acts 5:18-20) *"They arrested the apostles and put them in the public jail. But during the night an angel of the Lord opened the doors of the jail*

and brought them out. Go, stand in the temple courts, and tell the people the full message of this new life."

- Peter (Acts 12:6-8) *"Peter was sleeping between two soldiers, bound with two chains and sentries stood guard at the entrance. Suddenly an angel of the Lord appeared and a light shone in the cell. He struck Peter on the side and woke him up. 'Quick, get up!' he said, and the chains fell off Peter's wrists."*
- Paul and Silas (Acts 16:24-26) *"Upon receiving such orders, he put them in the inner cell and fastened their feet in the stocks. About midnight Paul and Silas were praying and singing hymns to God, and the other prisoners were listening to them. Suddenly there was such a violent earthquake that the foundations of the prison were shaken. At once all the prison doors flew open, and everybody's chains came loose."*

Jeremiah had been confined to the palace courtyard for several years – treated as a criminal – and his only crime was telling the people the truth. And while the people were ignoring his message – the events that Jeremiah predicted were taking place right in front of their eyes. Now the tables are turned: they are in chains – and He is free!

1. Why did all of the disaster happen to Jerusalem according to Nebuzaradan? (v.3)

   _____

   _____

God used the example of the disobedience of the Jews and the consequences of their disobedience to teach the surrounding nations as well as Israel.

Nebuzaradan then told Jeremiah that he was free to come and go as he pleased. If he wanted to, he could go to Babylon and be cared for, or he could choose to stay in Jerusalem.

2. "Look, the whole country lies before you (v.4)

   _____

   _____."

3. Then he recommended that Jeremiah go back and live with _____

    _____

    whom the king of Babylon has appointed over the towns of Judah.

4. What did Nebuzaradan give to Jeremiah before he let him go (v.5)?

    _____

    _____

5. Why do you think Jeremiah chose to stay in the land rather than go with
    the people to Babylon?

    _____

    _____

So Jeremiah went and stayed with Gedaliah, and lived among the people who remained in the land.

Read Jeremiah 40:7-12

Gedaliah took an oath to reassure the people and told the people he would represent them to the Babylonians. When the Jews who had been scattered to Moab, Ammon, Edom and all other countries heard that there was a remnant left in the land and Gedaliah had been appointed governor, they came back.

6. What did Gedaliah tell the people who were staying in Judah?
    *   Don't be afraid to (v.9) _____
    *   Settle down in the land, serve the king of Babylon and _____

        _____

    *   You are to harvest the (v.10)_____
    *   Live in the towns _____

Things appeared to be going well for the Jews who stayed in Jerusalem. As long as they obeyed the king of Babylon, they would live peacefully. God blessed their harvest with an abundance of wine and summer fruit.

WEEK SIX: DAY THREE – A NEW ENEMY

Read Jeremiah 40:13-41:1-3

Gedaliah was a very naïve man! He was warned that Ishmael was going to attempt to kill him, but he chose not to believe it, and not to take measures to protect himself. Gedaliah must have reasoned that he was such a good guy and had such good intentions that no one would want to harm him.

> *"A simple man believes anything but a prudent man gives thought to his steps."* Proverbs 14:15

> *"It is better to heed a wise man's rebuke than to listen to the song of fools."* Ecclesiastes 7:5

> *"Be on your guard against men."* Matthew 10:17a

Jesus said that we have an enemy who wants to harm us. The reason he wants to harm us is because God is his enemy, and we are the adopted children of God. The battle is not between satan and men, it is between satan and God. This battle began in the Garden of Eden and will continue until Jesus returns and throws satan into the lake of burning sulfur.

> *"And the devil, who deceived them, was thrown into the lake of burning sulfur, where the beast and the false prophet had been thrown. They will be tormented day and night for ever and ever."* Revelation 20:10

Sometimes satan appears disguised as a shepherd or sheep, or a hired hand.

> *"The thief comes only to steal and kill and destroy; I have come that they may have life, and have it to the full...The hired hand is not the shepherd who owns the sheep. So when he sees the wolf coming, he abandons the sheep and runs away. Then the wolf attacks the flock and scatters it....I am the good shepherd: I know my sheep and my sheep know me."* John 10:10, 12, 14

Just like it was foolish for Gedaliah not to believe someone would want to harm him, it is foolish for us to believe that the devil will leave us alone. Paul said,

> *"Keep watch over yourselves and all the flock of which the Holy Spirit has made you overseers. Be shepherds of the church of God, which he bought with his own blood. I know that after I leave, savage wolves will come in among you and will not spare the flock. Even from your own number men will arise and distort the truth in order to draw away disciples after them. So be on your guard!"* Acts 20:28-31a

How can we be "on guard" against the devil and his deceptive schemes? We need to stay close to Jesus, our Good Shepherd. We stay close by choosing to obey God instead of doing things our way (taking His yoke). We stay close by making prayer and bible study part of our daily routine.

We also need to keep our spiritual armor on: (Ephesians 6:14-18)

- *"Stand firm, then, with the **belt of truth** buckled around your waist*
- *With the **breastplate of righteousness** in place*
- *With your feet fitted with the readiness that comes from the **gospel of peace***
- *In addition to all this take up the **shield of faith** with which you can extinguish all the flaming arrows of the evil one*
- *Take the **helmet of salvation***
- *And the **sword of the Spirit** which is the **word of God***
- *And **pray in the Spirit** on all occasions with all kinds of prayers and requests"*

1. Who sent Ishmael to take Gedaliah's life? (Jeremiah 40:14)

_____

_____

The Ammonites had been enemies of Israel for centuries. Abraham's nephew Lot had two sons by his own daughters. The oldest was named Moab, the father of the Moabites, and the youngest was named Ben-Ammi, the father of the Ammonites. (Gen. 19:37-38) The relationship between Israel and the Ammonites and the Moabites became strained when Israel came out of Egypt and was returning to their homeland. In Deuteronomy, God gives the Israelites instructions on how they are to deal with the Ammonites.

> *"No Ammonite or Moabite or any of his descendants may enter the assembly of the Lord, even down to the tenth generation. For they did not come to meet you with bread and water on your way when you came out of Egypt, and they hired Balaam son of Beor ...to pronounce a curse on you. Do not seek a treaty of friendship with them as long as you live."*
> *Deuteronomy 23:3, 4, 6*

2. Who was killed by Ishmael along with Gedaliah? (41:3)

_____

_____

Read Jeremiah 41:4-15

There were eighty men who brought grain offerings and incense with them to the house of the Lord (which at this point had been burned down). We can assume these were God-fearing men who were grieving over the loss of the temple, and the city of David. They came from northern Israel – Shechem, Shiloh and Samaria. They tore their clothes, shaved off their beards and cut themselves to show the extent of their grief.

3. Where did all of these events take place? (v.1,3,6)

_____

_____

4. What did Ishmael do to these men? (v. 7)

_____

_____

5. What happened to the rest of the people who were in Mizpah? (v. 10)

_____

_____

6. Who saved the captives? (v. 13-14)

_____

_____

7. Where were they rescued? (v.12)

_____

_____

8. Who escaped and fled to the Ammonites? (v. 15)

_____

_____

The poor people who remained in the land were left with no governor, no officials, and no Babylonian soldiers to defend them. They must have felt very helpless and unprotected, like sheep among wolves. Jeremiah, however, was not worried. Like Paul the apostle, he believed that God would take care of both him and the people who were left in the land.

> *"So do not be ashamed to testify about our Lord, or ashamed of me his prisoner. But join with me in suffering for the gospel, by the power of God, who has saved us and called us to a holy life – not because of anything we have done but because of his own purpose and grace…. And of this gospel I was appointed a herald and an apostle and a teacher. That is why I am suffering as I am. Yet I am not ashamed, because I know whom I have believed, and am convinced that **he is able to guard what I have entrusted to him for that day.**"*
> *2 Timothy 1:8-9,11-12*

God promises all of us that He will guard what we have entrusted to Him.

9. What have you entrusted to God for His protection?

_____

_____

10. How can you be sure that you can trust God to guard what you've entrusted to Him?

    _____

    _____

"I have loved you with an everlasting love. I have drawn you with loving-kindness". Jeremiah 31:3

"'This is the covenant I will make with the house of Israel after that time,' declares the Lord. 'I will be their God, and they will be my people.'" Jeremiah 31:33

Our God is faithful to keep His Word. You can trust Him.

Week Six: Day Four – A Letter to the Exiles

Read Jeremiah 29:1-19 (a letter written after the 2nd deportation)

The letter began by reminding those in exile that God is still "the Lord Almighty, the God of Israel." He has not abandoned His people. He still holds all power, and is in control. God made it clear that it was Him that carried the people into exile in Babylon – not Nebuchadnezzar or his army!

God gave the people some instructions on how to live in exile. They should not think that they will be returning to the land of their forefathers anytime soon. God tells them to:

- Build houses and settle down
- Plant gardens and eat what they produce
- Marry and have sons and daughters
- Find wives for your sons and give your daughters in marriage
- Increase in number there, do not decrease
- Seek the peace and prosperity of the city to which God has carried them into exile
- Pray to the Lord for it (Babylon) because if it prospers, so will they
- Do not let the prophets and diviners deceive them

The letter tells the Israelites to seek peace and prosperity for the city to which God has carried them.

In a similar way, Paul wrote in his letter to Titus, that we must obey everyone who is in authority over us.

> *"Remind the people to be subject to rulers and authorities, to be obedient, to be ready to do whatever is good." Titus 3:1*

> *"There is no authority except that which God has established." Romans 13:1a*

1. Who are your authorities?

   _____

   _____

2. In what ways are you required by law to obey?

   _____

   _____

3. Do you always obey the authorities or just when you agree with them?

   _____

   _____

Then, God reminded them of the "seventy years" prophecy. (v.10) (See Week Three Day Three)

The last time Jeremiah had spoken about the "seventy years" in captivity was during the 4th year of King Jehoiakim's reign, about eight years earlier. Jeremiah now reminded the people that God was still planning to fulfill that prophecy. They would absolutely not be returning to Israel for the next seventy years, so they might as well settle down and get used to their new home.

What did God have planned for His people? (v. 11-14)

1. I have plans to _____ you and not to harm you.
2. I plan to give you _____ and a _____.
3. When you pray I will _____.
4. You will seek me and will _____ _____ me when you seek me with _____ your heart.
5. I will be _____ by you.
6. I will bring you back from _____.
7. I will _____ you from all the nations and places where I have banished you.

8. I will bring you back to the place from which I carried you into

_____.

God said He would bless the exiles with His love and comfort. He extends that same great love and comfort to us today. Jesus also told us that He would never leave us, and that we can look forward to our future with Him. When we are going through difficult circumstances like the Israelites in captivity, we can find assurances and comfort in God's Word. Today we might be facing hardship, but keep looking up! Our future looks very bright!

> *"I tell you the truth, you will weep and mourn while the world rejoices. You will grieve, but your grief will turn to joy. A woman giving birth to a child has pain because her time has come; but when her baby is born she forgets the anguish because of her joy that a child is born into the world. So with you: Now is your time of grief, but I will see you again and you will rejoice, and no one will take away your joy." John 16:20-22*

> *"Here I am! I stand at the door and knock. If anyone hears my voice and opens the door I will come in and eat with him, and he with me." Revelation 3:20*

> *"And he will send his angels with a loud trumpet call, and they will gather his elect from the four winds, from one end of the heavens to the other." Matthew 24:31*

> *"For the Lord himself will come down from heaven, with a loud command, with the voice of the archangel and with the trumpet call of God, and the dead in Christ will rise first. After that, we who are still alive and are left will be caught up together with them in the clouds to meet the Lord in the air. And so we will be with the Lord forever." 1 Thessalonians 4:16-17*

> *"For my Father's will is that everyone who looks to the Son and believes in Him shall have eternal life and I will raise him up at the last day." John 6:40*

Week Six: Day Five – The "Seventy Years" Question

Today we will try to better understand why God gave Jeremiah the "seventy years" prophecy. Why seventy and not one hundred? Did God randomly choose seventy years because it was a long time? The short answer is no. The seventy years of captivity is all about the land. Let's start at the beginning, when God created the earth in six days and rested on the seventh.

> *"By the seventh day, God had finished the work He had been doing, so on the seventh day He rested from all His work. And God blessed the seventh day and made it holy because on it He rested from all the work of creating that He had done." Genesis 2:2*

God made the seventh day holy. Then to make sure people understood just how holy it was, He included it as one of the Ten Commandments.

Read Exodus 20:8-11

God commanded the people to rest on the Sabbath. He also gave them specific Sabbath laws in the detailed instructions included in the Mosaic Covenant.

Read Exodus 23:10-12

The Israelites were commanded to let the land lie unplowed and unused every seventh year for the entire year. During this "Sabbath year", the poor among them could find food remains and wild animals could eat what was left. This was God's command, and He added a penalty to anyone who refused to let their land rest.

Read Exodus 35:1-3

1. What was the penalty for working on the Sabbath?

    _____

    _____

2. What else weren't they allowed to do on the Sabbath?

_____

_____

One consequence of not "lighting a fire" would be that there would be limited activities after dark. This encouraged them to retire early on the Sabbath, and wake up refreshed - ready to work hard the next day.

3. What kind of day was the Sabbath meant to be?

_____

_____

Read Leviticus 25:1-7

The Lord again commands the Israelites not to work on the seventh day or the seventh year. They must give the land a rest. (See verses 4-5)

Read Leviticus 25:8-23

God initiated a very special event, called a "Year of Jubilee", every fifty years. The Year of Jubilee would be celebrated the year after seven sets of seven years (49 years). It lasted for an entire year.

4. What were the people going to proclaim in the Year of Jubilee? (v.10)

_____

_____

The Year of Jubilee would be liberating! Everyone would return to his family property and each to his own clan. In the Year of Jubilee, all prisoners and slaves would be set free. All land deals would be valid until the Year of Jubilee, when everything would return back to its original owner. No permanent land deals could be made.

5. What were the people not to do in the Year of Jubilee? (v. 11)

_____

_____

6. What were the people going to eat if they did not plant or harvest any crops? (v. 21)

_____

_____

7. Why could the land not be sold permanently? (v. 23)

_____

_____

Read Leviticus 26:2-35

God wanted the land to rest. If the people insisted on planting and harvesting the land, he would have to remove them, until the land was completely rested.

8. Then the land will enjoy its (v.34) _____
    years all the time that it lies _____
    and you are in the country of your _____.
9. Then the land will _____ and
    _____its Sabbaths.
10. All the time that it lies (v.35) _____
    the land will have the _____it did not
    have during the _____ you lived in it.

Read Leviticus 26:43-45

What the people did not seem to understand was that God was not merely suggesting they could have a Year of Jubilee - He was commanding it. The Creator of the land, wanted the land to have a rest once every seven days, once every seven years for a full year, and then once again every fifty years for a full year. He promised to bless them with enough food to allow them to do this. But they would have to trust God to keep His Word. They would have to live by faith in God. He would be their Provider.

The Israelites did not keep the Year of Jubilee which was required by the terms of the Mosaic Covenant. There is no recorded account in Scripture of a "Year of Jubilee" taking place. In 1095 BC, Samuel the judge, anointed Saul to be the first king of Israel. So if you were keeping track (and God was) from the time of Israel's first king until the last king of Judah – Zedekiah (590 BC), there were 505 years. Over a period of 490 years, the <u>land would be entitled to 70 years of Sabbath rest </u>(one Sabbath year for every seventy years).

When the people were deported to Babylon, the land finally received its much-needed rest.

> *"The land enjoyed its Sabbath rests; all the time of its desolation it rested, until the seventy years were completed in fulfillment of the word of the Lord spoken by Jeremiah." 2 Chronicles 36:21*

WEEK SIX– SMALL GROUP DISCUSSION –
THE YEAR OF JUBILEE!

Open in prayer.

This week in Review:

1. Describe the details of the capture of Zedekiah and his officials. (Day One)
2. Describe Solomon's temple, and the significance of its destruction. (Day One)
3. Who set Jeremiah free, and where did he go? What was he given as he was released? (Day Two)
4. Who was Gedaliah? What lesson can we learn from his mistake? (Day Three)
5. What instructions did Jeremiah give to the people who were in Exile (in his letter)? (Day Four)
6. What is the Year of Jubilee? (Day Five)

The people of Judah were deported to Babylon and kept in captivity there for 70 years because they had not given the land its rest on the Sabbath Days, Years, and Years of Jubilee. (Every 7 days, every 7 years, and every 50 years) (Leviticus 26:33-35)

Let's consider what the Year of Jubilee means to us today.

Read Isaiah 61:1-11

Isaiah said that he was proclaiming "the year of the Lord's favor." What year was he referring to?

The <u>Commentary Critical and Explanatory on the Whole Bible</u> gives an explanation of this phrase:

> The "year of the Lord's favor" was the "acceptable year – the year of jubilee on which "liberty was proclaimed to the captives". (Jamieson, Fausset, and Brown, 1871, public domain)

Isaiah describes it as a year when captives will be set free and there will be a great celebration with gladness, praise, and comfort. This is a beautiful description of the Year of Jubilee.

In Leviticus God said if we observe His Sabbaths and have reverence for His sanctuary,

> *"I will grant peace in the land...and look on you with favor and make you fruitful and increase your numbers and I will keep my covenant with you. You will still be eating last year's harvest when you will have to move it out to make room for the new. I will put my dwelling place among you and I will not abhor you. I will walk among you and be your God, and you will be my people." Leviticus 26:6a, 9-12*

Now let's read a passage in the Gospel of Luke where Isaiah 61 is quoted.

Read Luke 4:16-21

Jesus said that He had come to "proclaim the year of the Lord's favor". Jesus further explained that in Him, this passage from Isaiah would find fulfillment. In other words, Isaiah was speaking prophetically of Jesus, and Jesus declared that He was the literal fulfillment of that prophecy.

The Spirit of the Lord (the Holy Spirit) was on Him – Jesus. (See Luke 4:1,14)

- To preach good news to the poor (see Mark 1:14-15, Luke 7:21-22)
- To proclaim freedom for the prisoners (see John 8:33-36)
- Recovery of sight for the blind (see Luke 18:40-42)
- To release the oppressed (see Luke 4:33-35)
- To proclaim the year of the Lord's favor (see John 17:1-3)

Take the time to look up each passage listed above. Jesus was declaring that there would no longer be a single "Year of Jubilee", but rather an Age of Jubilee. Once Christ offered his life in our place and took the full wrath of God on Himself, we would all be set free from the bondage of sin. We have been given freedom from sin, and sight from spiritual blindness. We have been given all of the riches of God's abundant grace. The keeping of the Sabbath and all of its laws and sacrifices were made obsolete with the coming of the New Covenant. Jesus said that He had come to preach good news – and this certainly is good news! Hopefully you and your group are grasping this awesome truth from God's Word. You have permission to let out a shout here!

Read Colossians 2:13-17, 1 Corinthians 15:21-26

7. What has Jesus Christ conquered? In a spiritual sense, we are all prisoners set free by Jesus. What have we been set free from?
8. Discuss what this liberty in Christ means to you.

Read Revelation 21:10 - 22:1-7

9. What will be the final fulfillment of the "Year of Jubilee"? (22:3-5)
10. Knowing that Jesus is coming back soon, how do you think He wants us to be preparing for that day?

"Because through Christ Jesus the law of the Spirit of life set me free from the law of sin and death." Romans 8:2

"Now the Lord is the Spirit and where the Spirit of the Lord is there is freedom." 2 Corinthians 3:17

"The creation itself will be liberated from its bondage to decay and brought into the glorious freedom of the children of God." Romans 8:21

As you end your small group discussion for Week Six, take time to pray for one another, encouraging and strengthening each other.

WEEK SEVEN

Off to Egypt

DAY ONE – THE REMNANT ASK FOR PRAYER

Read Jeremiah 42:1-22

The people came to Jeremiah and asked him to inquire of the Lord, what they should do. Should they stay in the ruins of Jerusalem, or go to Egypt? They want Jeremiah to ask God.

1. Who came to see Jeremiah to ask him to pray? (v. 1)

   _____

   _____

2. How long did the people have to wait for an answer? (v. 7)

    _____

    _____

3. What did the Lord want them to do? (v.10)

    _____

    _____

4. Was the Lord clear about what would happen if they went to Egypt? (v.16,18)

    _____

    _____

5. What would be the results of their disobedience? (v. 18)

    _____

    _____

6. In verse 20, Jeremiah says they made a "fatal mistake". What was it?

    _____

    _____

The people made a "fatal mistake". They asked God for His direction, then instead of following it, they did what they determined was best. They followed their own human wisdom and understanding.

Have you ever done that? Have you ever prayed about a matter, or read what God's Word says about it, then chose to do what seemed right to you instead? When we foolishly choose to do things our own way, the Bible says we are rebelling against God – just like the Israelites did in Jeremiah 42.

Read Proverbs 1:20-33

7. Name some of the things a foolish person will do. (v. 24, 25, 29)

    _____

    _____

8. Name some of the things a wise person will do. (v.23, 33)

   _____

   _____

9. When we ignore God's advice and reject His help, what will He do? (v.26,28)

   _____

   _____

"Dear friends if our hearts do not condemn us, we have confidence before God, and receive from Him anything we ask, because we obey His commands and do what pleases Him." 1 John 3:21-22

Read Matthew 7:24-29

10. According to the parable Jesus told in Matthew 7, what will you have to do in order to be a wise person? (v.24)

    _____

    _____

Sometimes we need to be reminded that God is the Sovereign Ruler over all mankind. He holds all power over heaven and earth. If we believe the notion that somehow we can control our own life and destiny, we are being led astray by the great deceiver. The truth is Jesus has been given all authority in heaven and earth. We would be wise to stay close to Him.

"Then Jesus came to them and said, "All authority in heaven and on earth has been given to me. Therefore go and make disciples of all nations, baptizing them in the name of the Father and of the Son and of the Holy Spirit, and teaching them to obey everything I have commanded you. And surely I am with you always, to the very end of the age." Matthew 28:18-20

Read Jeremiah 43:1-13

Jeremiah barely got the words out of his mouth, when Johanan, Azariah and all of the arrogant men accused Jeremiah of lying. They said that the Lord really did not say those things. God didn't really tell them not to go to Egypt.

1. Did these people – Johanan, Azariah and the others – have any proof or any reason to believe that Jeremiah was a liar?

   _____

   _____

2. Who did they accuse of inciting Jeremiah against the people? (v. 3)

   _____

   _____

Remember Baruch? He was a good friend who had written down the words as Jeremiah spoke them. He had been a close companion to Jeremiah over the past forty years, and had been allowed to remain in the land as one of the few that had not been deported. Now Johanan is accusing Baruch of inciting

Jeremiah against them. This accusation is unjustified. Baruch did nothing to deserve this.

There was nothing Jeremiah could do to stop them. Johanan and the army officers led the people off to Egypt. These were the very people who had recently come back to live in the land of Judah from the surrounding nations.

3. Who was led away in addition to the remnant of Israelites? (v. 6)

_____

_____

Tahpanhes, now Tell Defenneh, was a city in Ancient Egypt. It was located along a branch of the Nile River. This is the place where the remnant from Israel settled in Egypt.

4. What did the Lord tell Jeremiah to do in Tahpanhes? (v. 9)

_____

_____

5. Where was he to do this? (v. 8)

_____

_____

6. Who did God say He was going to send to Egypt? (v. 10)

_____

_____

7. What will Nebuchadnezzar do in Egypt? (v. 12)

_____

_____

8. What would be eventually placed over the stones buried in the entrance to Pharaoh's palace? (v. 10)

_____

_____

Notice that Jeremiah was able to give the exact location where Nebuchadnezzar would put his throne in Egypt. If Jeremiah was a false prophet, he would soon be exposed when Nebuchadnezzar came. But there is proof that Egypt did fall to Nebuchadnezzar just as Jeremiah prophesied, so the nations of the world should admit and recognize that Jeremiah spoke from God – and that the God of Israel is the one True God.

Proof of Egypt's fall to Babylon can be found in a clay tablet now in the British Museum which states:

> "In the 37th year of Nebuchadnezzar, king of the country of Babylon, he went to Mitzraim (Egypt) to wage war. Amasis, king of Egypt, collected [his army], and marched and spread abroad. **Having completed the subjugation of Phoenicia, and a campaign against Egypt** (*emphasis mine*), Nebuchadnezzar set himself to rebuild and adorn the city of Babylon, and constructed canals, aqueducts, temples and reservoirs."

9. Why was the Lord angry with Egypt? (v. 13)

_____

_____

Read Exodus 20:1-6

10. What is the first and greatest commandment? (v. 3)

_____

_____

Reflect on this commandment, as it applies to the current generation of people.

11. What are some of the gods that are worshipped today?

_____

_____

12. Have you ever owned an idol or participated in idol worship accidentally or knowingly?

_____

_____

Anything that we treat as though it had great value can become an idol. In the USA people worship movie stars, athletes, musicians and other celebrities. People go to fortune tellers, magicians, horoscope readers, and mediums for guidance. Rabbit feet, crystals, ouiji boards and games that promote death and demonic influence are completely accepted by people in today's culture. Many stores and homes have statues of Buddha or Hindu gods as fashionable decor. Statues of saints are also worshipped. Remember God said, "no other gods."

"Dear children, keep yourselves from idols." 1 John 5:21

Week Seven: Day Three – A Final Warning

Read Jeremiah 44:1-6

Jeremiah was now sixty years old. He had been prophesying for over forty years. His prophecies concerning Judah, Jerusalem, and the temple, had come to pass exactly as he had said. Now from Egypt, he reminded the remnant living in Egypt of all the disaster they had witnessed and why these things had happened.

Read Jeremiah 44:7-30

The remnant seemed determined NOT to obey the Lord. God, through Jeremiah, asks the people some questions:

1. Why bring such great disaster on yourselves?
2. Why provoke me to anger with what your hands have made?
3. Why leave yourselves without a remnant?

Don't you wonder why these people continued to do everything God told them NOT to do?

1. As a result of their disobedience, who would perish? (v.12)

   _____

   _____

2. What were the wives doing to provoke the wrath of God? (v. 17)

   _____

   _____

3. What reason did the women give for their actions? (v.18)

   _____

   _____

4. In v. 26, God says, "I swear by my _____ that no one from Judah living anywhere in Egypt will ever again invoke _____ or swear "as surely as _____".

5. What would be the sign to them? (v.29, 30)

_____

_____

God gave the Israelites many warnings and chances to do the right thing. They chose to disobey. They chose to do the very things that Jeremiah told them would provoke the wrath of God.

Hopefully we will make better choices than they did.

Read 2 Timothy 2:19-21

Choose wisely. Choose to be an instrument for noble purposes, useful to the Master.

"If anyone would come after me, he must deny himself, and take up his cross and follow me. For whoever wants to save his life will lose it, but whoever loses his life for me will find it." Matthew 16:24-25

The Death of Jeremiah

The Bible does not tell us when or how Jeremiah died. Several ancient writers, including Jerome and Tertullian (quoted by later historians), have written that Jeremiah died in Egypt. They agree that the Jews stoned him to death there, in Tahpanhes, the place that is last mentioned in the book of Jeremiah. Tradition says that he was stoned for denouncing the idolatry of the surviving Jews.

Read Jeremiah 17:13-18

1. How did Jeremiah describe the Lord in verse 13?
   - The _____ of Israel
   - The spring of _____

2. Fill in the blanks from verse 14.

- _____ me and I will be healed.
- _____ me and I will be saved.
- For You are the one I _____ .

In verse 16 Jeremiah tells the Lord, "I have not run away from being your shepherd." Jeremiah is implying that he was tempted to run, but didn't. He remained faithful even when it was extremely difficult. He then says (I'm paraphrasing), "Lord, you know...you understand...I haven't desired this day – this day of despair." And what "passed from his lips" every word he spoke - was open – not hidden from God.

Read Jeremiah 10:6-16, 23-24

Jeremiah said that out of all of the wise men in the nations, there is no one who compares to God.

Here is why God is so much greater than the other gods:

- He is more powerful (v.6)
- He is the eternal King, the Living God (v.10)
- He will not perish like the manmade gods (v.11)
- He created and founded the earth by His power and wisdom (v.12)
- He stretched out the heavens by his understanding (v.12)
- He makes the thunder, the clouds, the lightning, the rain, and the wind (v.13)
- He is the Portion of Jacob (v.16)
- He is the Maker of all things including Israel (v.16)

"He is the image of the invisible God, the firstborn over all creation. For by him all things were created: things in heaven and on earth, visible and invisible, whether thrones or powers or rulers or authorities; all things were created by him and for him. He is before all things, and in him all things hold together. And he is the head of the body, the church; he is the beginning and the firstborn from among the dead, so that in everything

he might have the supremacy. For God was pleased to have all his fullness dwell in him, and through him to reconcile to himself all things whether things on earth or things in heaven, by making peace through his blood, shed on the cross." Colossians 1:15-20

Paul described Jesus Christ as the Creator or Maker of all things. Paul, speaking through the Holy Spirit, said that Jesus has supremacy over all things. All the fullness dwells in Him. All things have been reconciled to Him in heaven and on earth. In other words, Jesus has all the power. He will never perish. He is Eternal. Paul was describing Jesus Christ – so was Jeremiah.

Jeremiah's entire life was devoted to God. He displayed a willingness to speak the truth boldly, defending God's Name, and enduring persecution for it. Jeremiah is an inspiration to all who claim to be followers of Jesus Christ. He was in the world, but not of it. He proved his faith, by his actions.

After forty years of preaching the Word of God, Jeremiah was ready to meet His Maker. He had fought the good fight. He had obeyed God. Now he would earn his reward.

Paul the apostle wrote to Timothy,

"I give you this charge: Preach the Word; be prepared in season and out of season; correct, rebuke and encourage - with great patience and careful instruction. For the time will come when men will not put up with sound doctrine. Instead, to suit their own desires, they will gather around them a great number of teachers to say what their itching ears want to hear. They will turn their ears away from the truth and turn aside to myths. But you, keep your head in all situations, endure hardship, do the work of an evangelist, discharge all the duties of your ministry. For I am already being poured out like a drink offering, and the time has come for my departure. I have fought the good fight. I have finished the race, I have kept the faith. Now there is in store for me the crown of righteousness which the Lord, the righteous Judge will award to me on that day – and not only to me but also to all who have longed for his appearing." 2 Timothy 4:1b-8

3. Both Paul and Jeremiah could say at the end of their earthly life that they: (2 Timothy 4:7)
   - Fought the good _____
   - Finished the _____
   - Kept the _____

4. Who also will receive the crown of righteousness from the Judge? (v. 8)

   _____

   _____

The Holy Spirit's words through Jeremiah and the Apostle Paul are an encouragement and motivate us to live a life of devotion to Jesus – who is the eternal King and the Living God.

> *"I have been crucified with Christ and I no longer live, but Christ lives in me. The life I live in the body I live by faith in the Son of God who loved me and gave Himself for me." Galatians 2:20*

"In the beginning was the Word, and the Word was with God, and the Word was God. He was with God in the beginning. Through him all things were made; without him nothing was made that has been made. In him was life, and that life was the light of men." John 1:1-4

Jesus Christ is the Living Word of God. He said that the Scriptures spoke of Him. When He came, He fulfilled the words spoken through Moses and the Prophets.

"And beginning with Moses and all the Prophets, he explained to them what was said in all the Scriptures concerning himself." Luke 24:27

For instance, as we carefully examined the book of Jeremiah, we found hidden references to Jesus as:

- Our Righteousness
- Our Covenant Representative
- Our Prophet
- Our Righteous Branch
- The Light of the world

- Our Hope for the future
- Our Potter
- Our Good Shepherd
- Our Sacrificial Lamb
- Our Suffering Messiah

- The Mighty Warrior
- The Judge
- The Name above all Names
- The Lord God Almighty
- The Truth
- Our Master
- Our Teacher and Guide
- Our Deliverer
- Our Redemption
- Our Justification
- The Stump of Jesse

- Offspring of David
- The Head of the Church
- The Initiator of the New Covenant
- The King of Kings
- The Vine
- The Eternal High Priest – Our Intercessor
- The Firstborn from the Dead
- Our Year of Jubilee – our Liberty
- The One and Only Living God
- The Word

Jeremiah is considered a forerunner of Jesus. A "forerunner" is "one that precedes and indicates the approach of another" (www.merriam-webster.com/dictionary). Today let's take some time to look at many of their striking similarities.

- Jeremiah and Jesus were both prophets who were not honored in their hometown. Compare Jeremiah 11:21 and Luke 4:24-30
- Jeremiah and Jesus were both called to tell the people about God's judgment on sinful people. Both predicted distress and destruction coming from God. Compare Jeremiah 7:32-34 and Matthew 24:21-22
- Jeremiah and Jesus both wept over the city of Jerusalem (also called "Zion"). Compare Jeremiah 8:21-9:1 and Luke 19:41-44
- Jeremiah and Jesus were both rejected by the religious and political leaders of their day. Compare Jeremiah 20:1-2 and John 18:3, 12-14
- Jeremiah and Jesus both were prophets to the nations, and not just Israel. Compare Jeremiah 46:1, 47:1, 48:1, 49:1, 50:1 and John 3:16,17, and Acts 1:8
- Jeremiah lived before and at the time of the destruction of Solomon's Temple. Jesus lived just before the Romans destroyed the rebuilt Temple. Compare Jeremiah 7:14, 52:13 and Matthew 23:37-38, 24:1-2
- Jeremiah and Jesus were falsely accused, arrested, and unjustly beaten. Compare Jeremiah 37:12-15 and Matthew 26:61, 27:26,30
- Jeremiah and Jesus were both rejected by the king. Compare Jeremiah 32:2-3, 36:26 and Luke 23:11

- Jeremiah and Jesus both were forced to go to Egypt because of persecution. Compare Jeremiah 43:6-7 and Matthew 2:13
- Jeremiah and Jesus both spoke the truth, and the words they prophesied, were fulfilled. Compare Jeremiah 29:10-14 and Matthew 26:2, 23, 31-32, 34
- Jeremiah was a priest from the family of Levitical priests who lived in Anathoth. Jesus was a priest after the order of Melchisedek from the tribe of Judah. Compare Jeremiah 1:1 and Hebrews 7:14-17
- Jeremiah wore a wooden yoke around his neck and was put in wooden stocks. Jesus was crucified on a wooden cross. Compare Jeremiah 20:2, 27:2 and Matthew 27:31,32

Many of the messages God spoke through Jeremiah were repeated by Jesus Himself.

- Jeremiah and Jesus both spoke about hypocrites and deceptive words. Compare Jeremiah 7:3-8, 9:8 and Matthew 15:3-9
- Jeremiah and Jesus both shared their disappointment and anger over the activity in the temple. Compare Jeremiah 7:9-11 and Matthew 21:12-13

- Jeremiah and Jesus both condemned the religious reinterpretation of God's covenant with the people. Compare Jeremiah 7:22-23, 8:8 and Matthew 23:1-3, 23-26
- Jeremiah and Jesus both taught about the New Covenant. Compare Jeremiah 31:31-34 and Matthew 26:27-28, Luke 22:20
- Jeremiah and Jesus both prophesied of a future that will be glorious. Compare Jeremiah 33:11 and Matthew 25:31-34

The Bible is a unique collection of inspired writings that span over a thousand years by different authors. As you compare the messages of Jeremiah and Jesus, it reveals a unity that binds the books of the Bible together. The same Holy Spirit that spoke through Jeremiah, also spoke through Jesus and each of the other writers of the Scriptures. Only an eternal God who knows all things, could write such an amazing cohesive book. Jesus is the Living Word of God.

We know that Jeremiah was an inspired man, anointed by the Holy Spirit and set apart by God. He willingly obeyed God and sacrificed his life for God. He was a good man.

Jeremiah **spoke** the Word of God.

> *"I will make my words in your mouth a fire and these people the wood it consumes." Jeremiah 5:14*

How can we compare Jeremiah to Jesus? We cannot. Jeremiah was just a man.

Jesus is incomparable. He is both the Son of God and the Son of Man. Yes, Jesus too was anointed by the Holy Spirit and set apart by God. He too willingly obeyed His Father and sacrificed His life for us.

But Jesus **IS** the Word of God.

> *"The Word became flesh and made his dwelling among us. We have seen his glory, the glory of the One and Only who came from the Father, full of grace and truth....From the fullness of his grace we have all received one*

blessing after another. For the law was given through Moses; grace and truth came through Jesus Christ." John 14, 16-18

"He exerted (his mighty strength) in Christ when he raised him from the dead and seated him at his right hand in the heavenly realms, far above all rule and authority, power and dominion, and every title that can be given, not only in the present age but also in the one to come. And God placed all things under his feet and appointed him to be head over everything for the church, which is his body, the fullness of him who fills everything in every way." Ephesians 1:20-23

1. Why is it impossible to compare Jesus to Jeremiah?

   _____

   _____

WEEK SEVEN– SMALL GROUP DISCUSSION –
Finding Jesus in Jeremiah

Open in Prayer.

Review:

1. Describe Jeremiah's character and personality.
2. Describe Jeremiah's relationship with God.
3. What have you learned about God's character through this study?
4. What have you learned about the Old Covenant – the Mosaic Law?
5. What have you learned about the Temple?
6. What have you learned about the New Covenant?
7. Who were the five kings that reigned during Jeremiah's life?
8. How many deportations were there and what do you remember about each one? (who was deported, what king was currently in power, what happened to cause the deportation?)
9. Why do some theologians call Jeremiah a "forerunner" of Jesus Christ?
10. Why is it impossible to compare Jeremiah and Jesus?
11. What are some of the differences between the times they lived in?
12. What lessons from this study have you been able to apply to your own life?
13. What did the Book of Jeremiah written 600 years before Jesus was born, teach you about Jesus?

The Rest of the Book......

If you have time, you may want to read and discuss Jeremiah's prophecies to the surrounding nations.

Concerning Egypt: Jeremiah 46:2-26
Concerning Philistia: Jeremiah 47:1-7
Concerning Moab: Jeremiah 48:1-47
Concerning Ammon: Jeremiah 49:1-6
Concerning Edom: Jeremiah 49:7-22
Concerning Damascus: Jeremiah 49:23-27

Concerning Kedar:	Jeremiah 49:28-33
Concerning Elam:	Jeremiah 49:34-39
Concerning Babylon:	Jeremiah 50:1-51:64

Congratulations! You have finished the study, and more importantly, you have studied the Scriptures, God's Holy Word. I hope that you and your small group have had a wonderful time of fellowship as you examined the Truth together. May you continue to find Jesus in the Scriptures, in your personal times of prayer, and wherever He reveals Himself to you through His Spirit. May God bless you with the "Spirit of wisdom and revelation, so that you may know him better." (Ephesians 1:17b) To God be the Glory!

Close in one final time of prayer for each other.

"I have loved you with an everlasting love; I have drawn you with loving-kindness. I will build you up again and you will be rebuilt." Jeremiah 31:3, 4

"The grace of the Lord Jesus Christ, and the love of God, and the fellowship of the Holy Spirit, be with you all." 2 Corinthians 13:14

ANSWERS TO THE DAILY QUESTIONS

WEEK ONE

Day One

1. the Israelites had sinned against the Lord by worshipping other gods and following the practices of the nations the Lord had driven out
2. Do not worship any other gods or bow down to them, serve them or sacrifice to them

Day Two

1. to confirm to the Israelites that they were His special people and He would be their God
2. those who are not with us today
3. bitter poison
4. It is because this people abandoned the covenant of the Lord, the God of their fathers, the covenant he made with them when he brought them out of Egypt.
5. the Lord uprooted them from the land in anger and in fury and in great wrath and cast them into another land

Day Three

1. the Lord will restore them from captivity, have compassion on them, and bring them back to the land again
2. the Spirit
3. from God
4. Someone who has had his heart circumcised by the Spirit
5. In the flesh
6. heart
7. those who are the children of the promise

Day Four

1. "Everything the Lord has said we will do."
2. Aaron, Nadab, Abihu, and 70 elders
3. they ate and drank
4. above the cover (mercy seat) between the two cherubim

Day Five

1. he rebuilt the high places, erected altars to Baal, added altars in the temple to the starry hosts, sacrificed his own son in the fire, practiced sorcery and divination, consulted mediums and spiritists
2. he tore his robes
3. To follow the Lord and keep his commands
4. They pledged themselves to the covenant

WEEK TWO

Day One

(Number of years that each king reigned: Josiah – 31 years, Jehoahaz – 3 months, Jehoiakim – 11 years, Jehoiachin – 3 months, Zedekiah – 11 years)

1. He was formed in his mother's womb
2. I don't know how to speak, I'm only a child
3. Do not say I am only a child. You must go to everyone I send you to and say whatever I command you. Don't be afraid of them for I am with you and will rescue you.
4. the disciples of Jesus
5. that he would be with them always, and would deliver them from any danger

Day Two

1. the branch of an almond tree
2. a boiling pot tilting away from the north
3. they will not overcome you and I am with you and will rescue you

Day Three

1. whole, Israel, Judah, my, renown, praise, glory
2. listen, hearts, gods
3. useless
4. that they would be to the "praise of His glory"
7. everyone curses him

156

8. God's words to him
9. the company of rebels – he never made merry
10. God's hand was on him and filled him with indignation
11. Repent and I'll restore you
12. a wall, a fortified wall of bronze, to deliver you, and I will redeem you

Day Four

1. marry, sons and daughters
2. funeral meal, sympathy
3. feasting
4. forsook, gods, worshipped, more wickedly
5. they are all going to perish
6. because God had withdrawn His blessing, His love and His pity
7. God is going to bring to an end the sounds of joy and gladness
10. God will restore them to the land that he gave their forefathers

Day Five

1. it was marred
2. he formed the clay into another pot
3. the house of Israel
4. he reserves the right to relent, or reconsider
5. It's no use. We will continue with our own plans
8. Slaughter
9. smashed, repaired
10. the court of the Lord's temple
11. all the people
12. Stiff-necked, would not listen to my words

WEEK THREE

Day One

1. God will relent
2. they said that Jeremiah must be sentenced to death
3. This man should not be sentenced to death. He has spoken to us in the name of the Lord our God.
4. Micah of Moresheth
5. King Hezekiah
6. we are about to bring a terrible disaster on ourselves
7. who Jesus was – if he was really the Messiah or not

Day Two

1. Magor-Missabib
2. Terror
3. fall by the sword of their enemies
4. Babylon
5. all the wealth of this city, products, valuables, treasures
6. go into exile in Babylon
7. die, buried
8. God

Day Three

1. Nebuchadnezzar, king of Babylon
2. 70 years
3. the king of Babylon and his nation will be punished for their guilt
4. the desolation of Jerusalem would last seventy years
5. Turned, pleaded, prayer, petition, fasting, sackcloth, ashes

Day Four

1. He is restricted and not allowed to go to the temple
2. the entrance to the New Gate
3. They looked at each other in fear and said we must report this to the king
4. they showed no fear, and didn't tear their clothes
5. arrest Baruch and Jeremiah
6. they made another scroll

Day Five

1. the exiles from Judah
2. God will watch over them for their good and bring them back, build them up, not tear down
3. Zedekiah, his officials and the survivors from Jerusalem
4. He will make them an offense to all the kingdoms of the earth, a reproach, an object of ridicule

WEEK FOUR

Day One

1. make a yoke out of straps and crossbars and put it on his neck
2. Edom, Moab, Ammon, Tyre, and Sidon

3. earth, people, animals
4. anyone
5. Nebuchadnezzar King of Babylon
6. wild animals
7. I will punish that nation with sword, famine and plague
8. your prophets, diviners, interpreters of dreams, your mediums or your sorcerers
9. remain in its own land to till it and to live there
10. King Zedekiah
11. they will be taken to Babylon

Day Two

1. two, the articles of the Lord's house, Jehoichin, all the other exiles from Judah

Day Three

1. perhaps the Lord will perform wonders for us as in times past so that he will withdraw from us
2. God Himself
3. die by sword, famine, and plague
4. surrenders
6.
   - it will be burned down
   - he will go to Babylon
   - he will die peacefully

Day Four

1. they accused him of deserting to the Babylonians
2. Is there any word from the Lord?
3. I will die there
4. He brought Jeremiah into the courtyard of the guard and gave him bread.

Day Five

1. Ebed-Melech, a Cushite
2. Yes
3. I will neither kill you nor hand you over to those who are seeking your life
4.
   - if they surrender
   - if they surrender
   - if they don't surrender
   - if they don't surrender

5. The Jews who have gone over to the Babylonians
6. Jeremiah might die

WEEK FIVE

Day One

1. Jesus Christ
2. The Lord their God and David their King
3. Peace and security
4. Devoured
5. Health, heal
6. Yes
7. God will make a new temple

Day Two

1. Israel and Judah
2. Forefathers
3. minds, hearts
4. my people
5. know
6. forgive, sins
7. Jesus lives forever, can save completely
8. The blood of Christ is unblemished and holy, able to cleanse us completely

Day Three

1. They have provoked God by all the evil they have done bringing in idols into the house of God, building high places for Baal, etc.
2. bring them back, I will be their God, singleness of heart and action, covenant, doing good, inspire, rejoice, good, heart and soul
3. have the faith of Abraham

Day Four

1. sit on the throne of the house of Israel
2. Only if we can break the covenant with the day and night so that they no longer come at their appointed time.

Day Five

1. abundant peace
2. joy
3. peace
4. joy, gladness
5. all understanding
6. hearts and minds
7. joy
8. glad

WEEK SIX

Day One

1. the temple, the palace, all of the houses, every important building
2. The rest of the poorest people of the land. Some of the poor had been deported.

Day Two

1. It was because the people sinned against the Lord and did not obey him.
2. Go wherever you please
3. Gedaliah
4. provisions and a present
5. Jeremiah had been living in captivity in Jerusalem. He now could come and go as he pleased, in the land that he loved. He could also be of service to the people who remained in the land.
6. Serve the Babylonians; it will go well with you; harvest the wine, summer fruit and oil; you have taken over

Day Three

1. Baalis, king of the Ammonites
2. all the Jews who were with Gedaliah as well as the Babylonian soldiers who were there
3. Mizpah
4. they were slaughtered and thrown into a cistern – all but 10 of them
5. They were made captives and led away to Ammon
6. Johanan
7. Gibeon
8. Ishmael and 8 of his men

Day Four

1. Prosper
2. Hope, future
3. Listen
4. Find, all
5. Found
6. Captivity
7. Gather
8. Exile

Day Five

1. Death
2. light a fire in any of their dwellings
3. a holy day, a day of rest to the Lord
4. liberty to all of the inhabitants
5. no sowing or reaping
6. God would bless them in the 6th year enough for 3 years so they would have enough left over for the Year of Jubilee, and also the next year.
7. because the land belongs to God and they are only aliens and tenants
8. Sabbath, desolate, enemies, rest, enjoy
9. Desolate, rest, Sabbaths

WEEK SEVEN

Day One

1. everyone from the least to the greatest
2. 10 days
3. stay in the land
4. yes – very clear!
5. God would pour out his anger and wrath, they would be an object of coursing and horror, condemnation and reproach, and they would never again come back to Israel
6. they asked Jeremiah to pray to the Lord, and said that they would do whatever he said
7. reject God; ignore God's advice and not accept His rebuke; hate knowledge and not choose to fear the Lord
8. respond to God's rebuke; listen to Him
9. God will laugh at their disaster; He will not answer when they look for Him, they won't find Him
10. Hear God's words and put them into practice

Day Two

1. No. Everything that Jeremiah had prophesied had happened exactly as he said it would.
2. Baruch
3. The men, women and children and king's daughters, Jeremiah and Baruch
4. take some large stones and bury them in clay
5. in the brick pavement at the entrance to Pharaoh's palace
6. Nebuchadnezzar
7. attack Egypt, bring death, set fire to the temples of the gods, take their gods captive
8. Nebuchadnezzar would put his throne over those stones, and spread his royal canopy above them
9. they had a temple to the sun, along with temples to other gods
10. you shall have no other gods before me

Day Three

1. all of them except a few fugitives (v. 14)
2. they burned incense to the Queen of Heaven and poured out drink offerings to her
3. ever since they stopped burning incense to the Queen of Heaven, and pouring out drink offerings to her, they have had nothing and have been perishing by the sword and famine
4. great name, my name, the Sovereign Lord lives
5. God would hand Pharaoh Hophra, king of Egypt over to his enemies

Day Four

1. Hope of Israel, Spring of Living Water
2. Heal, save, praise
3. Fight, race, faith
4. all those who have longed for his appearing

Day Five

1. Jesus Christ is the Word of God, the Almighty God, Creator of all things. He cannot be compared to any man.

BIBLIOGRAPHY

1. Scripture taken from the HOLY BIBLE, NEW INTERNATIONAL VERSION Copyright 1973, 1978, 1984 International Bible Society. Used by the permission of Zondervan Bible Publishers.
2. *Jeremiah the Fate of a Prophet. B.* Lau (2010) translated by S.Daniel, Koren Publishers, Jerusalem Ltd., www.korenpub.com
3. *Jeremiah a Drama in Nine Scenes.* S. Zweig, (1922) (This resource is in the public domain.) translated by E. Paul, Thomas Seltzer Inc., NY
4. *Exposition of the Old and New Testament.* J. Gill (This resource is in the public domain.) Osnova Kindle Publisher, www.osnova.com
5. *Rashi.* M. Liber, (this resource is in the public domain) translated by A. Szold; Jewish Publication Society of America
6. *The Power of the Blood Covenant. M.* Smith (2002) Harrison House, Tulsa Oklahoma www.malcolmsmith.org
7. *Commentary Critical and Explanatory on the Whole Bible.* R.Jamieson, A.R. Fausset, and D. Brown (1871) (This resource is in the public domain.)
8. *Bible Study Tools.* (2014) Salem Web Network, Salem Communications Corporation. www.biblestudytools.com

Printed in the United States
By Bookmasters